ROSES FALL

Roses Fall
Where
Rivers Meet

A Description and Explanation
of the
Shower of Roses
of the
Little Flower

by Father Albert H. Dolan, O. Carm.

St. Michael's Press
Charlotte, North Carolina

FIRST ST. MICHAEL'S PRESS EDITION 1995

PRINTING HISTORY
St. Michael's Press first edition published June 24, 1995
St. Michael's Press second edition published October, 1997

𝔑𝔦𝔥𝔦𝔩 𝔒𝔟𝔰𝔱𝔞𝔱   MATTHEW T. O'NEILL, *O. Carm.*
                              Censor Deputatus

𝔍𝔪𝔭𝔯𝔦𝔪𝔞𝔱𝔲𝔯   ✠ GEORGE CARDINAL MUNDELEIN,
                              Archbishop of Chicago

July 20, 1937.

Library of Congress catalogue number 95-69115

Cover design by Irene Lipton

St. Michael's Press
229 North Church Street • Suite 400 • Charlotte, North Carolina 28202

10 9 8 7 6 5 4 3 2

TABLE OF CONTENTS

AUTHOR'S PREFACE

THESE thoughts, first proposed at a novena at the Eastern Shrine of St. Therese in Englewood are presented here because so many who found them helpful urged their publication. If the wider reading audience finds in them inspiration and a more clear understanding of St. Therese, will they breathe a prayer to her to bestow upon the author a more generous share of her own unselfish love of God? He in turn begs the Little Flower always to keep them under her sweet protection.

The style in which the conferences were originally delivered has been, appropriately or inappropriately, preserved. The booklet has been titled "Roses Fall Where Rivers Meet" because its main theme is an explanation of the intercessory power of St. Therese. "The river which descended" and that which "remounted" blend now in a third stream of God's love which refreshes the world and which is known as "the shower of roses." May my readers participate abundantly in that shower of God's love and Mary's.

The basic framework of this booklet is a translation from the French. The author and title of the French original are unknown to me. The original French essays, on which this book is based, were published in a two or three-franc, paperbound pamphlet, which in 1926 I bought at a railroad newsstand in France. I was so impressed by it that for my own private use, I translated it during leisure moments on trains in Europe. The paper covers became worn and torn and finally, before I had made any note of the author and publisher, the pamphlet was lost. The pages of my translation remained and years later, when I decided to use the translation as the basis of this book, I endeavored in vain, through friends in France, to procure another copy, and to identify the author. Through this acknowledgment therefore I attempt to assign due credit to the unknown author from whom I borrowed generously, although I constantly departed from my own free translation of the original French. May St. Therese provide that the author of the original is abundantly rewarded for his share in whatever good this present book accomplishes in souls.

A. H. D.

Englewood, N. J.
Feast of Our Lady of Mt. Carmel,
July 16, 1937.

●

The Great Commandment

"Master, which is the great commandment in the law? Jesus said to him: Thou shalt love the Lord thy God with thy whole heart, and with thy whole soul, and with thy whole mind. This is the greatest and the first commandment. And the second is like to this: Thou shalt love thy neighbor as thyself" (Matt. 22, 36-39).

"THOU SHALT LOVE THE LORD, THY GOD, with thy whole heart"—these words of our divine Lord give the key-note to be stressed throughout our novena. We have announced that this novena would be in the nature of a retreat, a general retreat for men and women, young and old.

A Retreat

A retreat is a time of spiritual inventory, of self-examination, in which we plan that the future be more pleasing to God and more replete with happiness and peace and satisfaction to ourselves. The purpose of a retreat is to pluck the weeds that may have grown in the garden of our soul and to plant in their stead flowers of virtue that will bloom there and result in greater happiness and greater favor with God.

This novena, commemorative of the Little Flower's death, is a particularly appropriate time for such an inventory or retreat. During this retreat we shall take stock of our lives and of life in general, correct our perspective, drop all posing and pretense and find ourselves and be ourselves for a while. Shedding all rubbish and unessentials, we shall make a fresh start in the business of living well. All these things and more we shall attempt to accomplish during our novena.

During this novena we want to reach and help the following classes of men and women: good Catholics that they may become better; lukewarm, that they may become more fervent; sinful, that they may become true Catholics, loyal followers of Christ.

Lukewarm?

If, although you are not a great sinner, you are ashamed, in your heart, of the little you do for God and for His Church; if you are secretly disturbed sometimes when you realize that you are not one of those to whom your religion means everything, but rather one whose religion means little more than Sunday Mass; if you are disturbed when you realize that you are not one of those whose religion enters into and controls every department of your daily lives — if that description fits you, this retreat is for you.

Procrastinating?

If you are tied to some habit of sin, dishonesty, intemperance, lust, and have been postponing your return to God and resisting his warnings, if you are frightened sometimes when you think of the possibility of sudden death, but nevertheless lack courage to break with sin, then this novena is for you. It will supply just the courage you need to return to God, to restore your

Catholic citizenship and consequently regain your peace and happiness.

Unhappy?

If you are discontented and unhappy, if you feel that perhaps your religion should and could mean more to you and yet if you are afraid that your more complete surrender to God would interfere with your comfort, this retreat is for you. It will teach you the richness and happiness that our holy religion can bring into your lives. During this retreat then, open the windows of your souls and let the light and sunshine of God's grace warm and refresh and purify and strengthen you.

Ordinary Retreat Subjects

At first I had intended to speak concerning those subjects which are ordinarily considered in every retreat. What are those subjects? The four last things: Death, Judgment, Heaven and Hell. There are usually sermons also on Sin, on Confession, on Holy Communion. I had intended to treat these subjects separately under the patronage of the Little Flower and to use her words, especially her words during her last months on earth, as a basis for these talks.

A Study of Holiness

I have decided against that plan. Instead, throughout the novena we shall study St. Therese. We shall study her as we have never studied her before here, intensively, exhaustively. I shall give a series of sermons concerning her that I have long intended to give but always postponed because some whom I had consulted advised me that if I attempted to make clear the spirituality of St. Therese and her so-called "little way to heaven," I would be talking "over the heads of the people." I have decided that her spirituality and holiness can be so treated that it will not be "over the heads of the people"; so described that it will be clear to all and not only clear but interesting and supremely effective, effective in the sense that it will produce the effect which a retreat should accomplish, namely, spiritual improvement on the part of all.

We Rely Upon Her

Some one might object: "Those who
are making this retreat are not all good
Catholics; some are lukewarm; some are
sinners. How can you expect to affect the
sinful by a description of the high holiness
of St. Therese?" The answer is: (1) I do
not expect to affect them, but I do expect
St. Therese to do so. We will speak of her,
expose to you her very inmost heart and
propose her as a model, and she will do the
rest. She says herself: "The greatest elo-
quence cannot call forth a single act of sorrow or love unless grace touch the heart."
I depend therefore for the success of this
retreat not upon what I say but upon St.
Therese, in whose honor we are assembled
and who will obtain the grace each one of
us needs. (2) Leaving aside for a moment
the consideration of grace and of her intercession, I believe that no one, whether he is
fervent, lukewarm or sinful, can listen for
nine days to a description of what St.
Therese did for God without drawing a
contrast between her and himself and without being inspired by that contrast to do

more for God. Just how our study of
St. Therese will affect the fervent, the lukewarm and the sinner, will appear more
clearly later.

Lessons for All

I promise you, however, that as we proceed to study St. Therese there will be lessons for all of you, lessons that you will be
glad to have learned, and that in the process
of learning them you will take a degree of
interest and enjoyment that will be quite
unique in your experience, no matter how
many retreats or novenas you have made,
no matter whether you have never made
either before, and this simply because St.
Therese herself is so unique.

Amongst the effects of the study of her
spirituality will be: a realization of the
holiness which only the Catholic Church
could inspire; a realization that a life lived
for God is the only life that produces happiness; and a realization of the necessity
of certain virtues that we shall label "fun-
damental" and indicate as the "key-notes"
of our retreat.

CHAPTER TWO

The Three Rivers

WITH THAT PRELUDE WE ARE READY TO begin to outline our study of St. Therese. We begin it with the words of our text: "Thou shalt love the Lord thy God with thy whole heart . . . and thy neighbor as thyself."

Since that is our Lord's summary of a Christian life — love of God and love of neighbor — we may expect to find St. Therese remarkable for both, and those two phrases, love of God and of neighbor, sum up all the sermons of this retreat. Before we have finished, all such questions as these will be answered: How can a person really love God? Is not the phrase "love of God" a mere metaphor, a figure of speech? What does it mean? How can we really love God and, more particularly, how is it possible to love Him "with all thy mind and soul and heart and with all thy strength"? We shall see.

In order to demonstrate to you the Little Flower's love of God, it is necessary to show what God did for her as well as what she did for Him. It is true that God heaped His graces and divine favors upon her. But if He was immeasurably lavish with her, it is also true that she was immeasurably generous with Him. It was her generosity with Him that made her a saint and we may well make that thought one of the key-notes of our retreat: "Generosity with God in imitation of St. Therese."

When we study the Little Flower's love of God then, we must think of two great loves, flowing like two great rivers from their sources; one descending from the heart of God towards the Little Flower, and the other remounting from her heart to Him — two rivers, two magnificent streams of love (and we must not think of one without the other); and then we should imagine that these two streams eventually joined one another and, being blended, combine to pour their waters on all the world. This third stream of God's love is called "The Shower of Roses" — and may we drink deeply of this stream during this retreat, for we trust that its primary result will be for all of us a more generous love of God.

What I have said so far reveals the plan
of the three points we shall consider first
during our retreat: (1) that river of love
which descended; (2) that river of love
which remounted; (3) the blended and
combined waters of those two rivers which
are poured upon souls who wish to be
refreshed.

In our study of St. Therese we shall
first consider God's part in the making of
St. Therese.

Warning

Before proceeding further in our study
of St. Therese, it is necessary, as a prelude,
to fix firmly in our minds several facts
about her: (1) It is true that God bestowed
marvelous graces upon St. Therese, more
abundant graces than He gives to the ordi-
nary soul and this because He had special
work marked out for her, a unique mission.
(2) But it is also true that St. Therese was
free; she could have refused those graces,
neglected them, and in that case she would
not have become a saint. She became a
saint because she cooperated fully with the

graces God gave her (and that is one of the differences between her and ourselves; we do not fully cooperate with the graces and inspirations that God sends us). (3) Although it is true that St. Therese at birth was given by God certain marvelous qualities of mind and heart and soul that lent themselves easily to development into high holiness, nevertheless these same qualities could easily have made of her a great sinner if she had not used them only for God. (4) Moreover, she had the defects of her qualities in her childhood and to conquer these defects she was forced to wage the most constant and most relentless battle against self in the history of holiness, and in conquering them her struggles against self were as frequent as moments of the day and her victories over defects followed one another as swiftly as the seconds of time. She became a great saint because she completely conquered those faults.

It is necessary to keep all these facts in mind in our study of St. Therese. If we do not, we are likely to imagine falsely that God did everything for her and that she did little; or that she did everything and God very little. The correct understanding of St. Therese depends upon our keeping in mind that two forces explain her holiness: (1) the graces God gave her and (2) her cooperation with God's graces. With these facts in mind let us proceed with our study of St. Therese.

The image that I would have you constantly retain as we proceed is that of the three rivers, one descending, the second remounting, the third formed from the first two, and poured forth upon the world. In other words, we shall consider what God did for St. Therese, what she did for Him, and, finally, what they (God and St. Therese) as a consequence do for us.

The first stream we shall consider tomorrow.

PART TWO

THE FIRST RIVER: WHAT GOD DID FOR ST. THERESE

or

ST. THERESE, A MASTERPIECE OF GOD'S LOVE

CHAPTER THREE

●

God's Love Planned St. Therese

To make clear what God did for St. Therese, we shall consider that God planned her destiny, that God desired her and that in a sense God needed her.

Let us consider first that God not only planned her destiny but also desired and in a sense needed her. The creation and sanctity of St. Therese corresponded to a desire or, better, a need in the heart of God. In what sense can God need anything or anyone?

God Has No Needs

The answer involves some rather abstract, theological considerations, but I think I can make it clear to you. God has no needs in the sense that we have them. We are indigent by nature. God, being infinitely rich, is fully sufficient unto Himself. Being infinitely happy, nothing is lacking to His perfect happiness. This self-sufficiency is particularly true of His love, for His heart is an ocean without shores, a fathomless sea, a spring of love so prolific that He can, throughout the course of eternity, drink of His love without ever exhausting it. His own love of self suffices for God.

But every love has a natural tendency to expand, to communicate itself, to bestow itself; and the love of God, the greatest of loves, is no exception to that law. By His very nature, and in proportion to His immensity, He seeks to communicate Himself, to communicate His love, to bestow it upon others. And because God is infinite, there is, in that sense, in Him an infinite need to bestow Himself — to communicate

Himself. This need of course has nothing in common with that of a poor man who seeks from without and from others that which he himself lacks. God's need is the need of the rich man (of the *too* rich man), who, being unable to spend his wealth, seeks to scatter its excess. Similarly a super-abundant spring overflows. Similarly a fire, which is too intense, becomes a conflagration. All the needs of God come from the excess of His richness. It is for this reason that God's needs are infinite and you can understand therefore the immensity and the profundity of His desire to love His creatures and to be loved by them. That desire is infinite; it has no bounds nor limits.

God's Desire to Bestow His Love

There is a retreat thought which, if pondered, will profoundly affect our lives: *i. e.,* whoever you are, God's desire to bestow His love on you is infinite, boundless, and, whoever you are, His desire to be loved by you is also limitless. The entire purpose and plan of creation in God's mind is thus simply stated: To create men in order to

lavish His love upon them and to receive
their love in return. "Why did God create
you?" asks the little catechism. "To love
Him and serve Him in this world and to be
happy with Him forever in the next."

Likewise God became man to re-direct
towards Himself the heart of man, fallen and
glued to earthly loves. Our Lord was made
flesh to give God's own heart as the heart
of humanity. God became man in order
that after man had been regenerated and
sanctified by that Sacred Heart, God would
be able to receive from mankind more than
human love; in order that He might not
only be loved by us, but that He might love
Himself in each one of us; for the heart of
Christ beats in each one of us; we are members of Christ, joined to Christ, Who is the
head and heart of the Church of which we
are members.

What an immense glory would redound
to God if all human hearts, beating in
unison with His, returned Him love for
love, loving Him as He loves them, with a
generous love!

God's Love Rejected

But alas, the greater number of men reject Him, either refusing His love or bargaining with Him for their love, and therefore God, frustrated in His attempt, sees every day flowing back to Himself *unused* the stream of His Love which men would not accept.

God's Revenge

But it is characteristic of a great and generous lover never to admit defeat, just as it is impossible that the All-Powerful should ever be vanquished. And because He is infinite in love and in power, God knows how to take revenge upon an ungrateful world of men. But His vengeance is altogether loving and merciful.

What is His revenge, when the world refuses His love? This — in spite of the world, He creates hearts who love Him. In order to show that He is Master, He produces hearts who love Him whenever He wills and wherever He chooses. He selects them either from amongst the flower gardens of the world or from its muddy swamps. Thus the heart of a Magdalen, at the foot of the cross, beats in unison with that of the virginal St. John. He chooses for Himself the hearts of virgins and the hearts of mothers; the hearts of the single and those united in holy wedlock; the tender hearts of children and the robust hearts of men. He selects for Himself hearts amongst pagan and savage nations (as St. Rose of Lima or Catherine Tekakwitha) or He chooses them from amongst the most refined civilizations. He draws these hearts to Himself from amongst the ranks of the people as well as from royal palaces. And in choosing them, He gives to each whatever grace and love and perfection is necessary to enable each to correspond with his individual vocation and destiny. And in heaven nothing, after God, will be more beautiful to contemplate than the diversity of God's love in the hearts of the various saints.

A Unique Vocation

But in that multitude of ardent souls and of burning hearts, there shines out and will shine out brilliantly forever with a particular and unique splendor, the heart of St. Therese. For although all the other saints loved God ardently, nevertheless the love which gave perfection to their lives was not, in any other case but hers, their unique vocation. In some saints, their love of God took the form of penance; in others, the form of poverty. Their vocation was to perform penance or to exhibit the perfection of charity; the vocation of St. Therese was simply what she declares it to be, to love God. The love of the other saints took on various forms — they were apostles, martyrs, doctors, priests, penitents, founders of religious orders. But St. Therese had this unique privilege: **her vocation was Love.** Listen to her say so herself: "I have found my place in the bosom of the Church, and that place, O my God, You have given me. In the heart of the Church, my mother, I will be Love."*

---

* It goes without saying that whenever we speak of the *unique* love of St. Therese, we always except our Blessed Lady, the Co-Redemptrix. Such an exception St. Therese herself made (although she did not expressly state it because it was understood) when she said: "I desire to love our Lord as He has never before been loved."

Please be sure that you grasp this truth, for if you miss it, you will miss the whole secret of the mission of the Little Flower. Her unique and singular vocation is Love — to love God — to make Him loved by others. That was God's plan for the Little Flower. That was and is her vocation. So much for the explanation of in what sense God's love needed and desired St. Therese. She was, so to speak, a necessity of His love; she was further the instrument of His merciful revenge.

CHAPTER FOUR

God's Love Created St. Therese

God Planned a Loving Heart

NOW LET US CONSIDER A SLIGHTLY DIF-
ferent aspect of God's prevenient love for
St. Therese. In a century when the great
majority of men had only contempt for
God's advances and for His friendship, our
Lord determined to create for Himself a
heart which would love Him, and in which
He could satisfy His need to love and to be
loved. He planned to create a heart which
He could overwhelm with His love, by
which He would be loved in return and,
better still, a heart which would win to His
love a multitude of other hearts. He set
about to light a spark which would eventually enkindle and embrace the entire world.
St. Therese was that spark and we know
that the fire she enkindled is now world-
wide in extent.

God Planned a Childlike Heart

Where did God look for that heart? He
did not look for it in high places. He did

not direct His glance towards riches or power, or science or genius. He did not even address Himself to those who might be called giants of holiness. But he *lowered* His glance and it fell upon a child and there He fixed His choice. Why? The reason is very simple. For what is it that makes us admire the sun? It is because it illuminates the high mountain peaks? No, it is because it can send its light and its warmth to the smallest bits of moss hidden and lost in the lowest wooded valley. Similarly it is not astonishing that God should embrace the seraphim of heaven and the great souls of earth. His triumph is to abase Himself unto nothingness in order to transform that nothingness into Love. His glory is to transform littleness into a masterpiece of His Love.

God therefore sought the heart He planned amongst the hearts of the little and the weak, and His choice went directly to the heart of a child. Not to a child destined to grow up, but to a child who would, throughout life, retain the weakness and simplicity of childhood. Amongst a multitude of possible souls, He chose one which the Little Flower herself calls "a little soul," "a soul so little and so feeble that it would be, I think, impossible for God to create another more small, more weak." The story of St. Therese is described perfectly by our Lord's words: "O Father, Thou hast hid these things from the wise and prudent, and hast revealed them to little ones" (Matt. 11, 25).

God Planned a Humble Heart

At the time He created her, He provided that even when she should be loaded down with His graces, she would not thereby become a victim of pride and vanity, but would instead continually dig for herself new abysses of humility and thus attract ever more powerfully to herself the Holy Spirit, the Spirit of Love, Who has only to discover a soul empty of self, to pour out upon that soul in floods His treasures.

Behold then God's plan — a little, and very humble soul and the heart of a child. That is the material upon which God's hand is about to embroider a marvel of His love — a masterpiece of virtue and of grace.

God Executes His Plan

In the making of her, to show us what He could make of nothing, God put His Omnipotence at the service of His eternal Love. For that which is to distinguish this soul among a million will be her childlike love of God. Therefore it was only just that in creating her, God should act as a loving Father. And as a rich father does not count the dollars when giving a dowry to his daughter, so the All-Powerful God did not withhold His abundance in creating the soul of St. Therese.

God's great treasure is, so to speak, His heart. There the Holy Trinity, in the course of eternity, stores up for Itself love and felicity. From that store, God the Creator borrows whatsoever is noble and pure, grand and holy, to bestow upon the souls He creates.

God Gave Her All Forms of Love

Ordinarily when God creates a human soul, He gives to each the special form of

love which is consistent with His plans for
that soul — to one, virginal love; to another, maternal love; to one, tenderness; to
another, strength; to one, nobility; to another, devotion. But for the Little Flower,
one form of love only would not suffice.
To her, God gave all forms of love.

He gave her therefore the heart of a virgin,
and the heart of a spouse, with which to
love Him, the Spouse of Virgins, and He
inspired her to love Him as "He never
before had been loved." He gave her the
heart of a mother with which to love souls,
a maternal heart prolific enough to mother
a multitude of souls, big enough to embrace
all souls with her solicitude, souls of the
present, souls of the future. He gave her
the heart of an apostle, ardent enough to
desire to convert the world; the heart of a
priest, capable of sheltering the hearts of all
priests for whom she was to offer her convent life; the heart of a victim, who was to
take her happiness in sacrifice and self-
immolation. Finally He gave her the heart
of a martyr, who was to aspire to die a
martyr's death, with all its torments —

nay, more — who was not content unless she could suffer what all the martyrs suffered and who exclaimed: "Open, O Jesus, the book in which are written the deeds of all Thy saints and know that each one of these deeds I long to have accomplished for Thee."

Thus God brought together, as it were, all the great hearts of the great saints, and having assembled them, having put them together, He enclosed them in the little jewel box which was the heart of the child Therese.

God Gave Her Unique Power to Love Him

There is a poem, a fanciful one, in which the poet, thinking of the creation of a child, pictures God the Father as calling upon Mary to spin a tress for the child, and upon the angels to weave her hands of velvet flesh, and to tint her cheeks with roses from their wings, and upon our Lord to scoop the pools of paradise for her eyes and to place in each of them a star. Similarly we can imagine, although it is not mere fancy, that God wrought, not for the body but for the soul of St. Therese. Her soul was freighted with the love of God and she herself tells us that it was God Who placed it there. God gave her then a soul unique in its power to love Him.

God Adorns Her Soul

But a great love of God does not exist alone. It has company. It is accompanied by a splendid retinue of virtues and a brilliant escort of perfections. Thus in St. Therese God added to the qualities of heart, of which we have spoken, other excellences of character and of mind, in admirable proportion. In that childlike heart He placed the force and strength of a giant. He animated that heart with an invincible courage. To that mild little dove, He gave the glance of an eagle. He made of her an astounding medley of simplicity and of majesty; He gave her a keen mind, bright and penetrating, limpid as a spring and clear as truth, endowed with an extraordinary facility to express very simply and clearly the most profound thoughts of her heart. He made her somewhat of an artist and somewhat of a poet, but at the same time wise and judicious and prudent; her enthusiasm was tempered by the perfect equilibrium of all her faculties. The better to accomplish the designs of His love, He gave her an exquisite sensibility, and made her so fine and so sensitive, with an emotional equipment so vivid that, as a consequence, she was able to feel profoundly and to suffer much.

God Endows Her Body

Finally, God endowed her even with physical beauty. He clothed her with grace and charm, for He wanted her to be, He destined her to be, a little Queen of Love, conquering hearts, not by the force of arms, but by the sweetness of her voice, and by the suavity of her manner. And as a matter of fact, all those with whom I talked in France who knew St. Therese, spoke of a certain indefinable charm which emanated from her person, a charm, an expression in her eyes, which caused all to turn to look at her when, as a child, she passed along the streets of Lisieux; a charm that is reproduced in her authentic portraits and statues, a charm that has entered into many of our own lives and taken us captive.

All this is the masterpiece of nature on which, as upon a foundation, God built a masterpiece of supernatural grace. On this hearth so well prepared, God was to light the fire of divine love.

Because God did all this for her, she tells us in her AUTOBIOGRAPHY: "Your love, O my God, has surrounded me from my infancy; it has grown with me and now it is an abyss of which I cannot sound the depths."

CHAPTER FIVE

God's Love Prepared Her Place on Earth

WHAT I HAVE GIVEN, MY DEAR FRIENDS, IS a very feeble and inadequate sketch of St. Therese in so far as she was a masterpiece of God's merciful love. Later we shall speak of the Little Flower's cooperation with God. Thus far, please notice, we are considering God's part in the making of our saint.

Ordinarily God does not produce His masterpieces of love at one stroke. He prepares the sun in view of the future plant. He prepares nests for the birds. And He likewise prepares, long in advance, the cribs in which will be born His chosen ones. Ordinarily the saints are the reward of virtuous parents; God sends them as a blessing and a reward. And it is not rare that very soon after, the family line dies out, being incapable of producing anything greater or better. Thus the Martin line will perish, when the sisters of St. Therese, all nuns, will have died.

Two Saints Meet and Marry

Who were the father and mother whom God judged worthy to receive from His hands the little Therese, His masterpiece? Zelie Guerin and Louis Martin. When they were still single and very young, the world appeared too small for their great souls, and they aspired to quit the world and to embrace the religious life, to enroll under the white banner of virginity. But our Lord had other plans for them and His hand arrested them as they were almost on the threshhold of the cloister. They met and were married. They united their hearts and their virtues, and their home became the holy land where, thanks to the spotless purity of their lives, in an atmosphere of firm, vivid faith, and under the warm caress of the sunshine of the grace of God, Who reigned there as Master, there sprang up lilies, as the flowers bloom in spring.

These two parents renounced the glory of virginity only to give to God St. Therese and eight other virginal souls. At birth, all their children were promptly consecrated to God and God accepted their offering. To show His approval of their consecration to Him, in the case of four of them, He Himself bent down and with His own hands plucked their white flower-like souls to transplant them in the garden of heaven.

Her Sisters' Part in God's Plan

Eight children had already blessed their marriage before Therese, the little Queen, appeared. Queens are usually preceded by a cortège of honor. One cannot conceive of a queen without her court; similarly one cannot read attentively the Little Flower's AUTOBIOGRAPHY without picturing St. Therese as surrounded by her sisters. To fail to mention her sisters, as well as her parents, in speaking of God's graces to St. Therese, would be an injustice and would be to deprive the Little Flower of the source of the sweetest joy of her childhood.

God does nothing without reason and it was He Who marked out the part each sister was to play in the formation of the character of St. Therese. If there ever was a child who had need of sisterly affection it was Therese, and God provided all that was necessary. One sister, Marie, held her at the baptismal font; comforted her during the mysterious illness of her girlhood and at the hour of her bitter separation from Pauline; and prepared her for her first Communion. Another sister, Celine, whom she called "the sweet echo of my soul," shared all her little joys and little sorrows as well as her vast hopes and desires; and after the death of Therese, the artist Celine, by her brush, contributed in no small part to making her sister known. This little flower had need of warm affection in order to bloom fully in the garden of her home. This same sisterly devotion was to serve later on in the convent as a means of sharp mortification, when St. Therese, to prove her greater love of Jesus, frequently denied herself the company of her sisters.

God had further designs and plans. He knew that to guard and instruct and protect her during life and to make known and glorify His masterpiece after her death, there was also need of a sister who would have for her a love that would be more than sisterly, a maternal love, and from whom

Therese would have no secrets. That sister God supplied in the person of Pauline, of whom I have spoken so often, the second mother of the Little Flower.

The Family Circle

Moreover, to envelop her in a vast network of tenderness and to extend further the atmosphere of affection in which she was to blossom, God provided that there should be just beyond the intimate inner family circle that uncle and aunt who proved themselves so useful and so devoted, that it would be an injustice not to mention them here.

Do you begin to see how well God prepared everything that was necessary for St. Therese, that masterpiece of His love? He placed her in an environment of affection and piety. No wonder that St. Therese once wrote: "I do not understand the saints who do not love their families."

The family is the work of God and the grace of a profoundly Christian family is one of the greatest benefits that God can give a child. To the parents of St. Therese, after God, is due the sanctity of the Little Flower. It will be eternally their glory in heaven to have given to the world this "fine pearl," this rare treasure. An honor like theirs, however, must be bought and paid for—and the price they paid doubtless was the premature death of the mother and the sadness and suffering of the last days of the father.

Eternal Recompense Given Her Parents

Today, however, they rejoice in heaven, for they are the father and mother of an innumerable legion of souls, the legion of souls who follow the way of the Little Flower; souls who, having received so many graces through St. Therese, render their homage also to the mother and father she loved so well. This legion of souls will be the eternal recompense of those magnificently Christian parents, and in this we have a striking example not only of the good accomplished by Christian parents but also of the reward that God bestows upon them. "The generation of the righteous shall be blessed" (Ps. 111,2). In giving their daughters to God, they thought that their line would die out. But no; other children were born to them from many lands. "Thy sons shall come from afar, and thy daughters shall rise up at thy side" (Isa. 40, 4). There came to this father and mother, from the extremities of the globe, children who, indebted to St. Therese for many graces, render their thanks also to her parents and through them to God. Innumerable are those whom their "little queen" has converted or sanctified. Many owe to her the life of their souls. They are the children of her apostolate, the fruits of her martyrdom of love. Are not the Little Flower's parents their father and mother also, being the mother and father of her who saved them?

The Father of St. Therese

You have all seen the painting of the Little Flower asking, in the garden of their home, her father's permission to leave him to give herself to God. She, arms extended, seems to point in the distance to the Carmelite convent of her choice. And

in the gravity of his handsome countenance,
we can read not only the pain of his sacrifice but the joy that he experienced in
thinking of the honor God bestowed on
him in choosing, from his home, still
another spouse for Himself. We feel that
his reply was one that such a daughter
would expect from such a father, and instinctively we think: "O how good was
this father of St. Therese, another Abra-
ham, sacrificing his child and giving her to
us in giving her to Carmel."

May all parents making this retreat be
inspired to be equally generous with God
when He calls their children to Him either
to be priests or nuns. Let this be another
keynote of our retreat: Generosity with
God in imitation of the father of the Little
Flower.

Her Second Home

Her family home was not the only home
God prepared for St. Therese, His masterpiece of love. In the eternal plans of God,
the Carmelite nuns were to be her second
family and her second home was to be

the Carmel of Lisieux, the Carmelite convent which God had designed to be the crib
of many victims of His merciful love.

Carmel is par excellence the order of the
Blessed Virgin and it is to that convent
that, after having cured her, the ravishing
smile of the Blessed Virgin brought her.

Carmel is a home remarkable for the
delicacy of its love of God, for Carmel is
designed to atone for sin—to console, as it
were, our Saviour for His neglect and ill-
treatment at the hands of worldlings. And
that was precisely the vocation of St.
Therese, "To atone for sin; to console by
delighting the heart of her divine Spouse."

Carmel is also the home of zeal. Its coat
of arms bears the words: "With zeal am I
zealous for the Lord God of Hosts." In
Carmel the fire of apostolic zeal has always
burned brightly. There the Sisters immo-
late themselves incessantly. There they
pray, and with what ardor, for souls and,
above all, for priests. Oh, yes, it is easy
to understand that no other convent could
be better suited to the aspirations of the

Little Flower and to her mission and apostolate.

The great heart of the founder of that Carmel of Lisieux, St. Teresa of Avila, that great heart which beats in the hearts of all her daughters, that heart so human and yet so celestial, that heart in which nature and grace were so nicely blended, that heart in which the saint and the mother so harmoniously mingled, that heart of the great St. Teresa was more suited than any other to receive and shelter, when she left her father's home, the heart of the little Therese, for her heart also was great though little; grand yet simple; very human and therefore near and dear to us; very loving and therefore near and dear to God.

Therefore in assigning to St. Therese a place in Carmel, God's wisdom accomplished a two-fold object: (1) He enriched Therese with all the graces that the centuries had accumulated in the Order of Carmel; (2) He provided that the Carmelite Order should ever be resplendent with the glory of the name of St. Therese,

just as sunshine makes doubly resplendent
a palace already glorious.

Summary

To sum up then what we have said so
far: It was our Lord Who produced the
prodigy of sanctity whom we call the Little
Flower. Let us render Him the thanks that
are His due. Let us imitate her who was
always so faithful in attributing to God
everything that was good in her. You
remember what she said one day when some
one brought her a sheaf of wheat. Taking
one of the best ears, she said: "This ear
of wheat is the image of my soul. God has
loaded it with graces for me and others. I
wish always to humbly bend before Him
in acknowledgment of the abundance of
His celestial gifts."

Let us too then bend towards God in
humble and sincere gratitude. Let us thank
Him as she did and for her; let us thank
Him in our own name also, because the
graces God gave her are for us as well as
for her, for God made her so rich that she
might enrich us. Finally let us ask Him

that the grace which was so fertile in her soul may not be sterile, but fruitful, in ours, so that walking in her footsteps, following her little way, we may one day enjoy what she has these many years been enjoying, that peace and happiness which has no end.

Graces Fertile and Graces Sterile

In conclusion let me repeat the warning that we must never think merely of the graces God gave St. Therese; we must think at the same time of her cooperation with those graces. Of that cooperation and of the river of love that remounted from the heart of St. Therese to God we shall speak tomorrow. Today I have told you of the graces that God gave St. Therese and in this I had three purposes: First, that we may appreciate how thoroughly God prepared her soul for the unique mission He marked out for her in this world. Secondly, that we may read rightly the AUTOBIOGRAPHY of the Little Flower, on every page of which she expresses her thanksgiving to God for all He had done

for her. Thirdly and chiefly, I have described the graces God gave St. Therese in
order that we might notice, and apply to
ourselves, this truth: she did not waste
those graces of God, but *we* often do waste
the graces He sends us. In her soul, God's
graces were fertile; in ours, they are often
sterile. In her soul, His graces were fruitful;
in ours, they are often fruitless. In her soul,
those graces bloomed; in our soul, they
often wither.

Let no one say: "God did much for St.
Therese. He has not done so much for me."
The answer to that objection is that He
gives to each one of us the graces necessary
to attain a certain destiny He has marked
out for us and wishes us to attain. He
gives to each one of us the graces necessary
to acquire a certain degree of love of Him
and this degree of love and perfection He
desires us to acquire. Who is there here
who can say: "I am spiritually all that I
could be; I am exactly the kind of man or
woman I have planned for myself in my
most spiritual moments." There is no one
who can truthfully make that assertion,

and hence the necessity of learning from St. Therese to cooperate with all the graces of God.

God's Goodness To Us

Is it not true that upon us also He has lavished His graces? See all that He has done for us in His goodness! He has made us members of His Church. He has given us the graces that come to us through the sacraments and through the Mass. Think of all the graces and inspirations He sent us through the good homes in which we were brought up, through the advice and counsel and example of good parents and teachers, through, in many cases, a Catholic education, in which we learned the necessity of prayer and acts of religion. Think of the graces that have come to us through the pulpit, through the confessional, and through our Catholic reading and Catholic contacts, through the missions, novenas and retreats which we have so often made. And yet, in spite of all these graces, how much better are we than non-Catholics who have never received the graces of which I speak, who have not the sacraments, nor the Mass, nor the Church, nor missions, nor novenas, nor retreats?

Oh, in view of all these graces that we have received, let us not envy St. Therese her greater grace, but be grateful for our own abundant graces, and resolve that henceforth our lives will be more consistent with the generous graces God has given us as Catholics and that henceforth these graces will not be sterile but fertile and fruitful in our souls as they were in the soul of the Little Flower.

PART THREE

THE SECOND RIVER: WHAT ST. THERESE DID FOR GOD

or

THE LITTLE WAY OF THE LITTLE FLOWER

●

Prelude to Chapter Six

"Whosoever is a little one, let him come to Me" *(Prov. 9, 4).*

THERE IS DANGER THAT, IN CONSIDERING, as we have done, what God did for St. Therese, we might conclude that she, having received so much from God, deserves little credit or merit. That would not of course be a correct conclusion, for she would never have become a saint if she had not cooperated fully—yes, perfectly—with all the graces God sent her.

Having considered God's part in the formation of our little saint, we shall now consider her own part in her steady progress towards sanctity. In other words, we have considered that great river of love that descended from God to Therese and are now to contemplate that other magnificent stream of love that rose—remounted—from Therese to God.

Just as the waters brought from the sea by the clouds and deposited in the form of rain in inland streams, just as these waters tend to return to the sea by way of brooks and rivers, so the love that God deposits in the hearts of His creatures has a natural tendency to return to Him. The greater that love is, the greater is the strength of its tendency to return to God.

That is why St. Therese had early in life so great a desire to repay our Lord for the love she had received from Him. Even in her childhood she set herself to love God with all her power and strength. So true is this that we might almost say that her supernatural love of God was natural to her and that she loved her heavenly Father as babies love their fathers here below—by instinct.

Her Vaulting Ambition

How did she propose to repay Him? What was the extent of her aims? I could never make the magnitude of her ambition clear if she herself had not expressed it very simply. In her own words, her ambition was: "To love our Lord as He has never before been loved!" This audacity and boldness would have been presumptuous in a servant, or even in a friend, but was not blameworthy in a child, and that was her childlike ambition—to love our Lord as He had never before been loved! As she says elsewhere: "I desire to love Him to the point of folly." And again: "I desire to reach the highest summits of the love of God, to arrive at its perfection and plenitude."

No Complicated Methods

How was she to accomplish this ambition? In the presence of the numberless roads to holiness, any of which she might have chosen, Therese did not hesitate a moment. She did not entangle herself in complicated methods nor study learned

treatises. Guided by the instinct of her
heart, which she rightly felt would not
deceive her, she went directly to the source
of God's love. She decided to force an
entrance into the heart of our Lord, to compel Him to provide for the realization of
her loving desires. How? By what means?
She found her answer in the Gospel. In
turning over the leaves of that book which
she read so incessantly, she discovered its
sweetest, most profound secrets, those
especially that our heavenly Father con-
ceals from the wise and prudent of this
world but reveals to the little and simple
and humble. Above all she discovered this
Gospel truth: that to win our Lord one
had only to approach Him freely as a little
child. Little children He not only does not
reject but He calls them—He goes to meet
them. He takes them in His arms; He places
them upon His knees and embraces them
and presses them to His heart.

The Little Way

In her confidence and simplicity, little
Therese liked to feel that it was to herself

these words of Eternal Wisdom were addressed: "Whosoever is a little one, let him
come to me" (Prov. 9, 4). From that time
her road to holiness was plainly marked
and her resolution was taken: namely, to
become a little child in the arms of the good
God, to go to her heavenly Father as children here below approach their fathers, to
love Him as they do theirs and to make
Him love her as His child. In other words,
the little way of the Little Flower, about
which so many learned volumes have been
written, may be simply and clearly expressed thus: **Her little way consists in passing her life in giving and receiving love from
our Lord, without any other occupation than
to please Him.** Then, after a life employed
in winning His smile, she would pass from
His arms into His heart, to lose herself
there forever in the furnace of His love and
to become there eternally the happy victim
of His love.

That is very simple, but it is a complete
description of the little way of spiritual
childhood. It is indeed as *old* as the Gospel, but nevertheless, by the individual and

original manner in which she conceived and practiced it, she made it a *new* way, to which she gave her name, "My *little* way" —a way that is very sure and very rapid, and which conducted her in a very short time to the highest summits of Love; a luminous and attractive way by which she wishes to captivate a legion of souls.

That we follow it ourselves, my dear friends, is her wish. Even to study it will edify us and be of profound spiritual benefit. So let us study in detail her secret of holiness. Let us observe her closely; let us watch her to learn how she entered upon this little way, how she progressed upon it and how she became perfect in it.

Three Elements

There are three chief elements in her little way: humility, confidence and love. We enter her little way through the door of humility; then we walk or, better, fly on the wings of confidence; and finally we are perfected by the virtue of love. These three virtues, these three essentials of her little way, we shall study separately.

CHAPTER SIX

The First Element of Her Little Way: Humility

ST. AUGUSTINE, WHOSE GENIUS ILLU-mined with lightning flashes so many truths, has a beautiful and powerful thought on humility. He says: "Here is an astonishing truth: God is the Most-High God, but nevertheless if you exalt yourself, He will depart far from you; but if, on the contrary, you humble yourself, He will come down to you. Why? Because, being so exalted above the heavens, He looks from His heights with love upon what is lowly, rather than upon what is magnificent. He looks askance at pride in order to humble it and He looks favorably upon humility in order to elevate it."

These words of St. Augustine may well be taken as one of the key-notes of our retreat. And the same thought is more concisely expressed in these words of our Lord Himself: "He that humbleth himself shall be exalted and he that exalteth himself shall be humbled." Behold in these words the reason why our Lord, when on earth, so loved little children; it was precisely their littleness which gave them the place they occupied in His heart.

A Beacon-light

This truth, notice well, my dear friends, was one of the great beacon-lights that illumined the life of St. Therese.

With her clear vision, she understood well that if she wished to approach God closely, it would be necessary for her to become a child, remain a child, and make herself very small. But what does that mean—to make oneself little? It means to be humble. To be altogether little means to be altogether humble. To be humble means to recognize one's littleness, to love one's littleness and be pleased with that littleness. That we *are* little; that we have all the frailty and weakness that go with littleness is true; and humilty is not pretense but truth. Let us dwell upon that point for a while.

Mistaken Notions of Humility

Humility is a virtue which many misunderstand. It is true that the world admires a man who is modest about his attainments; it can appreciate a man who does not brag, who seems unconscious of his gifts and talents and honors. It rather approves a man who can bring himself to treat inferiors as equals. But these are only some very superficial and exterior manifestations of a kind of humility which may exist in a man who is not humble at all in a Christian sense.

The world does not understand deep, interior Christian humility and has an entirely erroneous view of what real humility is. In fact it regards Christian humility of the Gospel as mere snivelling mean-spiritedness, if not downright hypocrisy. Worldlings think that humble people are pious posers, devout make-believers (as when the Little Flower says that everything good in her she owes to God); they think that to be humble a man must shut his eyes to his own virtues. This is an entirely false view of humility. St. Therese herself writes illuminatingly on this truth. She says:

"If a little flower could speak, it seems to me that it would tell quite simply what God had done for it, without hiding any of its gifts. It would not say, under the pretext of humility, that it was not pretty and had not a sweet scent, that the sun had withered its petals or the storm had bruised its stem—if it knew such were not the case.

"The Flower now telling her tale rejoices in having to publish the wholly undeserved favors of our Lord. She knows that in herself she had nothing worthy of attracting Him; His mercy it was that filled her with good things—His mercy alone."

Humility Compatible with Self-assertion

No, a man can be humble and still recognize his own virtues. The humble man does not close his eyes to what is good in him, but he refers what is good in him to God and therefore does not become proud of his attainments. So the world is wrong when it judges that humility is affectation, hypocrisy or make-believe. Those Catholics are wrong too who think that humility is antiquated, incompatible with modern hustle and bustle, that it is not an up-to-date virtue. An examination of lives of successful but humble Christian men and women would disclose that humility is even compatible with self-confidence and self-reliance and even, on occasion, compatible with self-assertion—these qualities may exist side by side with true humility.

Definition of Humility

Having disposed of some of the mistaken notions of humility, let us, without further prelude, define what humility is. Humility is truth. The basis of humility is truth, the truth about ourselves. Humility is based on true self-knowledge. Anyone who knows the truth about himself will be humble. The man who is proud does not know himself. "If any man think himself to be some thing, whereas he is nothing, he deceiveth himself" (Gal. 6,3). Let us try to realize that truth. As we read over our

life's history we shall find many blank
pages and numerous soiled ones, and we
shall probably be mentally jolted by the
discovery that self is really equal not to
something, but to less than nothing, equal
to minus zero. "What have you that you
have not received?" asked St. Paul. Let us
answer this question for it will give us true
self-knowledge.

What have you that you have not received from God? As regards material
goods, gifts of body and mind, and gifts of
soul, we must answer with a sweeping
negative St. Paul's question: "What have
you that you have not received?" How
humiliating is the answer: "Nothing; absolutely nothing. All that I have is from
God."

These considerations should fill us with
distrust of ourselves, fill us with humility,
fill us with self-scorn at our unwarranted
pride. And filled with this newly-born
humility, we should go to God during this
novena, and every day of our lives, and

humbly acknowledge our own nothingness, our own utter dependence on Him. Only in such humility can we enter upon the little way of the Little Flower.

A Fascinating Truth

A humble view of oneself is offensive to many proud souls, and it is more unpalatable the more proud one is. But instead of offending St. Therese, this truth had for her an invincible attraction and completely fascinated her mind and heart: it fascinated her mind, which Nature had made so limpid and straight and true that she valued nothing but the truth; it fascinated her heart that our Lord modeled after His own heart, making it meek and humble.

Crib and Tabernacle

Hastening to follow in the footsteps of our Lord, she pursued Him chiefly where He reveals Himself as most humble and small and little—namely, in the crib and in the tabernacle, for it is in Bethlehem and in the Blessed Sacrament that our Lord

becomes little, annihilating Himself for love
of us.

"The Kings of the earth are men of might,
    And cities are burned for their delight,
But the King of Heaven, Who made them
    all,
Is fair and gentle, and very small;
    He lies in the straw, by the oxen's
    stall."

Having considered Him in His humility
in the crib and tabernacle, she exclaimed:
"Oh, my Well-Beloved, Thy example invites me to abase myself; to despise honor
and to win Thy love, I wish to remain ever
little and humble."

Notice, my dear friends, how she mingles
love with petition for humility. Such is
the power of God's love upon her little soul
that she cannot, in the spiritual life, take a
step or make a gesture or utter a word or
form a project which is not inspired by
divine love. Doubtless she wished to remain little because she was convinced of
her littleness in God's sight, but how much
more because she wanted in her love thus

to please our Lord. It is as if the heart of the Christ Child, with its thirst for humiliation, had taken the place of her heart and dwelt there in her. The phrase that summarizes the earthly life of our Lord, summarizes her life: "He emptied Himself." To this the Little Flower responds: "Therefore I must remain little and become ever more and more small."

"He emptied Himself"—behold another key-note or slogan of our retreat: to empty oneself of self, of self-will, of self-seeking, is at once the way to happiness, the way to humility, the way to greater friendship with God, the way to heaven, the little way of the Little Flower.

Constant Practise

That is why everything that lowered her in her own estimation, pleased her. And this not only in theory but in practise. She practised constantly — I mean just that, *constantly*—the virtue of humility, renewing again and again each day the practice of humbling herself in thought, in word and in deed. With little children, weakness and littleness are two sisters who never leave each other. No one is more feeble than a very tiny child. Therefore Therese's love of weakness went hand in hand with her love of littleness! Her AUTOBIOG-RAPHY is filled with these avowals of her helplessness, as, e.g., the following words taken from her AUTOBIOGRAPHY: "I do not distress myself when I see my utter helplessness; on the contrary, I glory in it." She tells us that the light God sent her to reveal to her her own nothingness did her more good than His lights on matters of faith. Again she says: "The All-Powerful God has done great things for me and the greatest is to have shown me my own little-ness, my powerlessness to accomplish any-thing good."

A child is not only small and weak; it is also poor. Even the child of rich parents possesses nothing of his own. He receives everything, day by day, from the hands of his father and mother. And since that trait of dependence characterizes children, St. Therese determined to acquire it herself. One cannot read her AUTOBIOGRAPHY without seeing what a joy it was to her ever to depend for everything upon her heavenly Father; to be nothing, to have nothing of herself; to be obliged to rely upon Him for the smallest things, even for help to accomplish the smallest act of virtue. As for the merits that she gained by her prayers and sacrifices, she kept none for herself. She gave them all to our Lord "to buy souls." Thus the more poverty-stricken she became, the more contented she was.

But where does such conduct lead? To abase oneself, to impoverish oneself, where does it end? You have probably guessed already, if you have recalled the promise of our Lord: "Whosoever humbleth himself shall be exalted." I need not relate, because you know, how this promise was verified in the history of St. Therese.

CHAPTER SEVEN

The Second Element of Her Little Way: Confidence

A Vision of Beauty

IN ANNOUNCING THIS NOVENA OR RE-
treat I said that I believed that no one,
however lukewarm or sinful, could listen
for nine days to a report of what the Little
Flower did for God without being profoundly affected spiritually and without
being inspired in some measure to imitate
her. And to-day, and perhaps more especially to-morrow, there will be presented
to you, in our analysis of the spirituality
of the Little Flower, a vision of spiritual
beauty and loveliness that is quite unsur-
passed and irresistible in its power to inspire
those who have the faintest spark of spirituality. Incidentally that vision of beauty,
which is the heart of the Little Flower, has
through the years drawn a very great number of men and women into the Church of
God, which alone can inspire, foster and
perfect spiritual beauty and loveliness.

To-day we are to speak of the second element of the little way of the Little Flower: her confidence in God.

A child who possesses nothing, who can do nothing for himself, looks to his father instinctively for everything. So St. Therese, voluntarily impoverished, turned towards her heavenly Father to confide to Him her helplessness.

Definition of Confidence

Confidence means more than hope; more than faith; it means absolute trust, deep-rooted trust which admits of no misgiving; trust in God as a good and kind, merciful and gentle Father.

How Her Confidence Was Acquired

How did St. Therese acquire her trust in God? We saw yesterday how well she understood that to win God's love she must draw very near to Him, approaching Him as a very little child. Since her very littleness led her to the arms of her Father, nestling down there near His heart, she listened to Its beatings, and each one of Its throbs seemed to say to her: "Child, My Child. If you only knew how I love you. If you only knew how much good I desire you to accomplish—Look! . . ." And then she imagined God proving, as it were, to her that He loved her in spite of His awesome power.

"Look," she imagined God said to her, and in her heavenly Father's hand the child saw the universe, which He poised with ease in the palm of His hand, as we would, in ours, a grain of sand. Nestling there in the arms of her heavenly Father, St. Therese saw, as it were, one of His fingers trace for the stars the courses they were to take across infinite space, courses from which they do not swerve; and she saw Him fix in the sand the line across which the sea is not permitted to pass. She saw in His eyes an expression that sees all things; on His forehead a wisdom that wisely disposes all things; in His arms power governing all things. And while she looked, wonder of wonders, she saw His hand caress her lovingly; His eyes smile upon her; she watched wonderingly while the All-Powerful One covered her with the mantle of His love. She heard that great God address her as "My child," and she answered Him, "O, my good Father!"

And that which no earthly child has ever experienced in the arms of the most powerful and most tender of fathers, she enjoyed near the heart of her heavenly Father—namely, the happiness there is, when one has nothing and can accomplish nothing, the happiness there is in feeling oneself entirely enveloped by God's love as tender as it is strong.

Unnecessary Fear

In thus thinking of God, the Little Flower was correct, for He is no tyrant to inspire fear, but a Father with a father's love for each of us, and that lesson of confidence it is her mission from God to teach us.

When St. Therese felt the embrace of her heavenly Father, all fear disappeared from her heart. That fear of God which is born of sin and is the result of sin, and which we find in the heart of sinful humanity (and which explains why so many cannot readily comprehend the high spirituality and familiarity with God manifested by the Little Flower), all that fear of God vanished; it evaporated in the warm sunshine of God's love as revealed to St. Therese. Thereafter St. Therese always viewed all the attributes of God in the light of His merciful love. To her, all the divine attributes shone with His love. I say, *all* the divine attributes, including His justice, and His justice more than the others. That is the reason she wrote: "I know that God is just and that His justice affrights many souls, but, instead of frightening me, His justice gives joy and confidence." Then she explains: "Because to be just means not only to show severity towards the guilty, but also to recognize our good intentions and our weakness. It gives me joy to think that God is just, because that means that He knows all our weaknesses and all the frailty of our nature and takes them into account."

Infinite Mercy

In the domain of His Infinite Mercy, therefore, God permitted her to enter like a queen into her own palace. He spread out His mercy before her and conferred it upon her as a kind of mantle. He bestowed upon her the power of understanding the mystery of His tender and boundless mercy, so that she could teach it to others and induce others to taste it and experience it, so that there would be no more fear of God, which keeps so many from Him, Who ought to be and is towards all of us, the kindest of kind Fathers.

What a fortunate child! Into this most priceless treasure of the treasures of God, into His mercy she can now dip; with full hands she can borrow His mercy for us.

She told herself that she must not leave the delicious place she had found against the heart of God, knowing that if she departed an instant, she would find herself poor and desolate indeed. She warned herself against pride. She understood that the least complaisance she took in herself would dry up or at least diminish the flow of grace into her soul. She knew that before throwing herself into God's arms she had been weakness itself, and that it would be so again, if she left those arms. She understood also that for her own good, her heavenly Father would permit perhaps that she fall into some very little imperfections, some very little faults. She was not surprised at this. But she told herself: "At such times a glance of confidence towards my Father will suffice to raise me up and restore me." And thereafter if she fell into some little infidelity, instead of flying from God, she would press closer to His heart.

God's Riches Are for Us

Thereafter nothing — absolutely nothing—could disturb her peace and her confidence. That is why I said in announcing this novena that during it we would learn that if we imitate St. Therese and follow her little way of spiritual childhood we shall enjoy the peace that she ever experienced. Nothing could disturb her peace, for knowing that she was the child of a Father infinitely rich and infinitely good, she concluded correctly that the infinite treasures of her Father were for her. Instead of fearing to demand too much of God as we do (because we judge Him by ourselves and measure His power and His goodness by our own), instead of making that mistake, she reminded herself that the treasures of God are inexhaustible, that He gives as He pleases without measuring, without ceasing, and that what He gives does not impoverish Him but that, on the contrary, there is always more to give; that the more we ask the more He is pleased, and that He is a thousand time more desirous of giving than we to receive.

Snow and Roses

St. Therese understood that a rich father refuses nothing to the daughter he loves. Therefore, just as she did not hesitate to ask Him for snow on the day of her profession (the day of her espousals, through her vows, with His divine Son), so she did not fear to ask Him, on the day of her meeting with Him in heaven, for a shower of roses to let fall on earth.

What sublime and admirable confidence in the heart of God! Everything yields before that confidence. And as she obtained her snow, so she obtained her shower of roses—her shower of roses for us. **That shower of roses, notice well, is a result of her childlike confidence in God.** That shower includes the gift to us of greater confidence in God.

I have described to-day the Little Flower's trust in God in order that we too may approach God with trust and confidence. Let us learn from St. Therese to-day that God is good, that His mercy is boundless, that we need have no fear of Him, that we should go to Him like little children as she did, trustfully, confidently, depending upon Him utterly. Upon the wings of such confidence we shall fly — we shall not merely walk — along the Little Flower's way to heaven.

CHAPTER EIGHT

The Third Element of Her Little Way: Love

WE PASS NOW TO THE CONSIDERATION OF the third element of the little way of the Little Flower, the virtue of love. Herein we shall find the very heart of the Little Flower. Do not be surprised that the confidence of the Little Flower had so complete a sway over the heart of God, for love pleaded her cause. It was her love of God, as well as her confidence, that caused God to give her her snow and her shower of roses. It would be a mistake to believe that confidence, even confidence based on humility, would suffice to force the door of the treasury of heaven. That which renders a child so persuasive with its parents is its love.

God Not a Tyrant

To understand her love of God, it is necessary to put aside, once and for all, all false and erroneous conceptions of God — those which picture Him only with thunder in His hand, or which represent Him as so

great and so distant that we scarcely feel
that we have the right to look towards
Him, and to say, more through obedience
than through affection, "I love Thee."

God is a Father

No, above all else and before all else,
God is a father. He is a father from all
eternity. Even before being Creator, he is a
father. By His very nature He is a father;
and His paternity, theologians tell us, is
the principle of His life and the source of
His happiness. Again theologians tell us
that in God all joy springs from this that,
having eternally generated His only Son,
perfect like Himself, He can give to Him
and receive from Him, perfect love.

God Desires Filial Love

He is father also to the creatures He
creates. He is still more truly a father when
He communicates to men **grace,** which is
part of His own life and which makes man
a participant in the life of God. Not only
is God a father but nothing pleases Him
more than to be treated as a father and to

receive from His children expressions of their truly filial love.

It was this truly filial, daughterly love that St. Therese had for her heavenly Father. All her life she was to Him a little loving daughter, occupied with pleasing Him and charming Him by her love for Him expressed in word, thought and deed.

Her Longing to Return His Love

But let us consider, my dear friends, to what perfection she brought her love. Hers was a heart of exquisite tenderness and therefore she desired to return God love for love. She realized that His love for her was immeasurable, infinite, but nevertheless she longed to return His immeasurable love as far as it was humanly possible. There is an exquisite passage in her AUTOBIOG-RAPHY, in which she expresses this desire to love Him as He had never been loved. She writes:

"To be Thy spouse, O my Jesus, to be a daughter of Carmel, and by my union with Thee to be the mother of souls, should not all this content me? Yet other vocations make themselves felt, and I would wield the sword, I would be a Priest, an Apostle, a Martyr, a Doctor of the Church, I would fain accomplish the most heroic deeds — the spirit of the Crusader burns within me, and I would gladly die on the battlefield in defence of the Church.

"The vocation of the Priesthood! With what love, my Jesus, would I bear Thee in my hand when my words brought Thee down from Heaven! With what love, too, would I give Thee to the faithful!

"Like the prophets and doctors, I would be a light unto souls. I would travel the world over to preach Thy name, O my Beloved, and raise on heathen soil the glorious standard of the Cross. One mission alone would not satisfy my longings. I would spread the Gospel in all parts of the earth, even to the farthest isles. I would be a missionary, but not for a few years only. Were it possible, I should wish to have been one from the world's creation and remain one till the end of time.

"But the greatest of all my desires is to win the martyr's palm. Martyrdom was the dream of my youth, and the dream has only grown more vivid in Carmel's narrow cell. Like Thee, O my Adorable Spouse, I would be scourged, I would be crucified! I would be flayed like St. Bartholomew, plunged into boiling oil like St. John, or like St. Ignatius of Antioch, ground by the teeth of wild beasts into a bread worthy of God.

"With St. Agnes and St. Cecilia I would offer my neck to the sword of the executioner, and like Joan of Arc murmur the name of Jesus at the burning stake. Open, O Jesus, the Book of Life, in which are written the deeds of all Thy Saints: each one of those deeds I long to accomplish for Thee."

Would Give Her Life Bit by Bit

But she was only a little child, capable only of little things. Moreover, she was shut up in a Carmelite convent. Brilliant deeds were therefore denied her. She could not spend herself in proof of her love, like the missionary, in apostolic labors. She could not die, like the martyrs, for the Lord she loved. "Very well," she said, "not being able to give my life to Him all at once, I will give it to Him **bit by bit, moment by moment.**" That is, in **each one** of her actions, even the most insignificant, she determined to express her love; in **each one** of her actions she would put her whole heart, on fire with love for God Who was so good to her.

Expresses Her Love in Each of Her Actions

But her determination is best expressed in her own words. If we would understand her method of expressing her love of God, let us listen to her own description of it. The passage I am about to quote follows one in which she tells us that she asked herself how, since love is demonstrated by deeds, she could prove her love? She answers in this surpassingly beautiful paragraph from her AUTOBIOGRAPHY:

"But how shall I show my love, since love proves itself by **deeds?** I, the little **one,** will strew flowers, perfuming the Throne of God with their fragrance. I will **sing** Love's canticle in silvery tones. Thus will

my short life be spent in Thy sight, O my
Beloved! To strew flowers is the only
means of proving my love, and these flowers will be each word and look, each little
daily sacrifice. I wish to make profit out of
the smallest actions and do them all for
Thee. For Thy sake, I wish to suffer and
to rejoice; so shall I strew my flowers. Not
one flower that I see but, singing all the
while, I will scatter its petals before Thee.
Should my roses be gathered from amid
thorns, I will sing notwithstanding, and the
longer and sharper the thorns, the sweeter and
more melodious will be my song."

Let us beware, my dear friends, of allow-
ing ourselves to be captivated merely by the
charm of these enchanting words. This is
not mere poetry. Let us dwell thoughtfully
on these words and they will reveal in all
its beauty the great soul of little Therese.

First let me add this other passage, which
clarifies and completes the one I have
quoted. She writes to her sister Pauline:
"I want to give all to Jesus — all. Everything shall be for Him."

Lets Pass No Opportunity to Express Her Love

Indeed it is impossible to go further in the giving of oneself. This "everything for Jesus," practised **unceasingly,** requires a soul alert for every occasion to humble herself, forget herself and sacrifice herself, in order to give pleasure to God — at **all times.** For she would not and did not let pass any opportunity for a little sacrifice — not one. Not one! Ah, that means more than appears at first thought. It requires reflection to realize what it means — a day, a week, a month, years without letting pass a single opportunity to do something, however little, for God.

Literally Incessant Acts of Love

That means constant, incessant acts of love and sacrifice which, with St. Therese, were actually as frequent as the seconds of time, for each second brought with it a new opportunity and she would not let one escape. These little sacrifices, little deeds of love, taken singly amount to little, but when we consider that they succeeded one another as the water flows out of an inexhaustible fountain, ah, then what constant application they suppose, what perfect self-renouncement, what generosity, what heroism! Are you beginning to understand the holiness of St. Therese, the depth of her love, the perfection of her little way?

Singing All the While

When we have stated that she did everything for our Lord, have we said all? No, we have not yet sounded the depths of her love of God. We have not yet noticed the most touching part of her declaration of love; we have not yet entered the most moving phase of our analysis of her little way of love. Let us occupy ourselves with it now. The supreme delicacy of her gift to God was not "to give everything to Jesus," but to give everything to Him with a smile, as if it cost nothing — with a smile even when the sacrifices were most painful. The supreme delicacy of her gift was, as she tells us, "to sing all the while, even when my roses are gathered from amid thorns, and the longer and sharper the thorns, the sweeter and more melodious will be my song."

Never Refused Him Anything

These, my dear friends, are not mere empty words springing from an emotional heart in a moment of enthusiasm. They are a very summary of the life of St. Therese. These words actually summarize her life: "To sing all the while, even when my roses are gathered amid thorns, and the longer and sharper the thorns, the sweeter and more melodious will be my song." She lived those words, before she wrote them. She lived them day after day, week after week, year after year. For one day, in speaking confidentially to her sister, she said, not proudly but very humbly: "From my childhood, I have never refused the good God anything." Never refused the good God anything! Try now, my dear friends, to understand a life — an entire life — spent in the practise of such love of God. It is indeed love remounting to its source. All that God had given her, she returned by her little way of sacrifice, by the continual, incessant gift of self under the form of her perfumed petals. Here was a life given bit by bit, moment after moment, to God.

Proposes to Offer Self as Victim of Love

But still we have not sounded the depths of her love. The great heart of the angelic Therese was not yet satisfied. Her love of God increased with the years and she experienced the torment, felt by all the saints, of feeling her powerlessness to repay a love that was infinite. In St. Therese this torment was increased by the thought of the refusal of so many men to accept the love God offers them. Therefore she determined to love Him for all those who do not love Him. She resolved to divert into her own soul, and absorb, the floods of divine love which others refused. She resolved to love God in their place, to love Him with their hearts; and, better still, she resolved that in order to atone for their ingratitude, and also to supplement her own weakness, she would borrow from God His own heart to love Him with. She would appropriate Its flames; she would not only love Him, but be transformed into His love; she would live and die of love.

This point is a little difficult, but it will become clear in a moment. The boldness of a child accomplished what would have been impossible to the powers of a giant. It inspired her to offer herself as a **victim** to God — as a victim to His merciful love — as a victim to be consumed in atonement for the sins of those who neglect, refuse or spurn God's love.

Preparation for the Offering

Already the childlike Therese had prepared the way by lavishing her tenderness and her flowers upon the heart of her Father. Already she had captivated Him by her caresses. But to take Him captive no longer sufficed. She desired further to be His captive and to compel Him to bring her to the center of the furnace of His divine love. She boldly asked that His divine arms should become her "elevator"; that Jesus should fascinate her with His eagle-like gaze, that the darting flames of the divine furnace should consume her. For her part, she would be content meanwhile to remain little and feeble, knowing well that "the weaker one is, the more acceptable one is to the operations of Consuming and Transforming Love." "Abandon," complete surrender, would be her sole law; the will of God, her unique pleasure. And her activity meanwhile would be merely to be faithful to Him. While her Father was carrying her up, she would not cease to smile upon Him and to scatter for Him her little flowers.

On the 9th of June, 1895, when she was twenty-two years old, on the Feast of the Holy Trinity, she offered herself as a victim of God's love, to be consumed by His love in atonement for men's indifference to His love. Her offering follows:

"O My God, O Most Blessed Trinity, I desire to love Thee and to make Thee loved. I desire to fulfil perfectly Thy will, and to reach the degree of love Thou hast prepared for me in Thy kingdom. I offer to Thee all the merits of my Saviour and of all the saints in heaven and on earth, together with their acts of love, those of the holy angels, and the love and the merits of the Blessed Virgin, my dearest Mother — to her I commit this oblation, praying her to present it to Thee. I cannot receive Thee in Holy Communion as often as I should wish; but art Thou not all-powerful? Abide in me as Thou dost in the tabernacle—never

abandon Thy little victim. I long to console Thee
for ungrateful sinners, and I implore Thee to take
from me all liberty to cause Thee displeasure. If
through weakness I should chance to fall, may a
glance from Thine eyes straightway cleanse my
soul, and consume all my imperfections — as fire
transforms all things into itself. I wish to labor
for Thy love alone—with the sole aim of pleasing
Thee, of consoling Thy Sacred Heart, and of sav-
ing souls who will love Thee through eternity.
In order that my life may be one act of perfect
love, I offer myself as a holocaust to Thy Merciful
Love, imploring Thee to consume me unceasingly,
and to allow the floods of infinite tenderness gathered up in Thee to overflow into my soul, that so
I may become a martyr of Thy love, O my God!
May this martyrdom one day release me from my
earthly prison, after having prepared me to appear
before Thee, and may my soul take its flight —
without delay — into the eternal embrace of Thy
merciful love! O my Beloved, I desire at every
beat of my heart to renew this oblation an infinite
number of times, till the shadows retire, and ever-
lastingly I can tell Thee my love face to face.
Amen."

Result of the Offering

Those of you who are acquainted with
her life know what new and immense graces
followed her offering on that Trinity Sunday. The will of God became in truth her
only pleasure, her sole law. If possible, she
was more faithful, more constant than

before in scattering her flowers and in smiling as she gathered them amidst thorns. From that Trinity Sunday, the love of God seemed to penetrate and possess her; destroying, if indeed there was need, any traces of imperfection; animating all her actions, even the most indifferent. There was no imperfection left in her. She had reached the heights — the highest summit of perfection — in the practise of the virtue of love. The love of God consumed her as the flame consumes the oil of a lamp, or better, it consumed her after the manner of a conflagration which consumes and yet ever seeks more to consume.

She Realizes Her Dream

St. Therese had attained her ambition, realized her dream — which was to live of love, and to be consumed by love, and there remained but to die of love, and that dream too was realized, as we shall see. God refused her nothing and He therefore granted her the grace of dying the death of love she had so ardently desired. In what sense she died of love, died a martyr, we

shall see in detail later. Let it suffice now
to say that she expired in an ecstasy of
love, with these last words of love upon her
lips: "O — how I love Him . . . My God,
I . . . love . . . Thee."

She is Our Guide and Leader

I know that you have all been deeply
moved at this glimpse of the heart of St.
Therese. It would be impossible for anyone with the least spark of spirituality to
remain unmoved as he looks deeply into
the great and loving heart of our little
saint. But that emotion which moves us is
worthless unless it is translated into deeds,
unless we take her as our guide and walk in
her footsteps along her little way. She wants
us to follow that little way of hers—wants
us all to follow it. You have seen how God
granted her least desires. He will grant too
her desire, which is His also, that we follow
her.

To Love a Little and then Much

She will lead us gently, but will firmly
force us, though ever so sweetly, to follow
that little way; to become little as she was

in the presence of our heavenly Father; to go to Him confidently, humbly, lovingly, as a child to its good father; to love Him at first a little and then much; to seek, by our fidelity to daily duty always accomplished for love of Him, to imitate St. Therese gathering and scattering her flowers; to do what we can for God's Church; to perform the tasks of our state of life, whether these tasks include beds or dishes, typing or drudgery, to perform these tasks smilingly as so many expressions of our love of our Father and Saviour and Friend; bearing pain, tolerating disagreeable relatives and boresome surroundings — all for love of Him. Unless we try to do that, we are not true followers of the Little Flower. She will provide that during this retreat we all make a beginning, howsoever small.

If you feel already the desire to begin, ask her to strengthen that desire lest it become weak and sterile in you. If you lack courage to begin, ask her for it; she will not refuse.

If you thus summon the courage to commence, she will see you to your destination, and walk hand in hand with you, to support and strengthen and to cheer you with her ever-present, unfailing smile.

Holiness a High Adventure

Thus, in our own small way, we shall begin our march towards holiness. **Holiness is the highest of high adventures, the grandest achievement in the world and the most desirable.**

And upon that note I shall close, reminding you that if there is one thing that our study of the life of St. Therese should teach us, it is that her little way is easy, and is open to all of good-will, however weak and feeble they may be, and indeed the more weak and feeble they are, the easier it will be to begin to perform the *little* acts of virtue which constitute the little way of the Little Flower. We may not be able to crowd into our lives as many of these little acts as she did, but we can make a beginning, and in that beginning there is some holiness and I repeat, as one of our retreat slogans, "Holiness is the highest of high adventures, the grandest achievement in the world and the most desirable."

PART FOUR

THE THIRD RIVER: THE MISSION OF ST. THERESE

or

THE LOVE WHICH SHE CAUSED TO FLOW UPON THE WORLD

CHAPTER NINE

●

Roses Fall Where Rivers Meet

"He that believeth in Me, the works that I do, he also shall do; and greater than these shall he do. Because I go to the Father and whatsoever you shall ask the Father in My name, that will I do: that the Father may be glorified in the Son" (John 14, 12-13).

Rivers Meet

WE HAVE RECENTLY DESCRIBED THE river of love that descended from God to the heart of St. Therese and the river of love that remounted from her heart to God. Now we are to consider that when these two streams met, their blended waters were poured out upon the world. In other words, we are to consider the mission of St. Therese after her death.

God in His wisdom uses men for the execution of His works in this world and makes men not only the beneficiaries but the instruments of His power and mercy. I have said "instruments," for the most powerful of humans, left to himself, can do nothing without God, nothing without Jesus. The more dependent upon God a person is, the more facile an instrument of God he is and the more capable of great things.

Therefore God, wishing to work wonders through the instrumentality of St. Therese, commenced by establishing her absolute dependence upon Him, by uniting her to Himself by the bonds of His divine love.

Roses Fall

Since He desired through her to shower roses upon the world, He commenced by planting her, so to speak, as a rose bush of love in the depths of His own heart. And the graces which St. Therese now scatters in profusion upon the world budded in the bosom of God's divine mercy before they passed through her hands. Her roses are, above all, flowers of Eternal Love.

An Astounding Spectacle

Because He used and is now using St. Therese as such an instrument, we behold to-day a spectacle truly astounding: that of a multitude of every race and sex and age and condition in life, at the knees of the little Therese, their eyes fixed upon her. Some are thanking her; others are petitioning her; all are exalting her power and goodness; all are relying upon her for favors for themselves, for the Church, for their country, for the graces proper to their particular state in life. And from on high, unwearyingly her hand gives and gives and gives.

A Second Lourdes

One cannot count the sick, the afflicted, the troubled, the tempted, the souls that aspire to the Christian ideal of living, who have sought her help and seek it still. There

is no physician, no lawyer, no man of
affairs, who has so many clients as she.
There is no director of conscience so celebrated. There is no other to whom so many
souls look for direction to perfection. Her
fame has spread to the most remote villages
of the globe. Her tomb is the most fre-
quented of the century, and the little town
in which she lived, so unknown before her
coming, has become a new city of miracles,
a second Lourdes. On Fifth Avenue in New
York City the other day I saw, in the window of one of our chief travel bureaus, a
placard reading: "Lisieux, World-wide
City of Pilgrimage" ("Lisieux, Centre
Mondiale de Pelerinage").

Roses Fall Where Rivers Meet

If we seek an explanation of all these marvels, it is to be found in what we have been
for some days explaining, in that stream of
love which descended from God to her heart
and returned to Him to be poured out upon
the world.

You will find an explanation of it also
in these words of our Lord: "He that be-

lieveth in Me, the works that I do, **he also shall do** . . . because I go to the Father and whatsoever you shall ask the Father in my name, that will I do: that the Father may be glorified in the Son" (John 14, 12-13).

Given Extraordinary Power with God

The humble Therese indeed **believed in** Jesus. She believed not only in His power but in His love. In the simplicity of her confident faith, she seized upon the very letter of His divine words, and as the Father glorified Himself in His Son, so she asked our Lord that she might spend her heaven as He spent His life on earth, doing good. She asked the Father and the Son to glorify not her but Themselves in her, Their little child. And just as the Father gives all power to His Son, so won by the love of this little child, God, just as He promised, gave to her an **extraordinary power over His heart.** As a matter of fact, the marvels of the history of St. Therese, of which we are living witnesses, are nothing else but God's power placed at the disposition of a child.

Given a Unique Mission

God does not thus act with all souls, not even with all those privileged souls whom He most tenderly loves. We are dealing with a fact that is altogether singular, altogether exceptional, altogether unique, and which corresponds to an equally singular destiny which God marked out for St. Therese. In other words, she has from Him a unique mission to accomplish in the world, and now we are to explain that mission and to state in what it consists. That will be our subject today.

Proofs of Her Mission

For anyone acquainted with the facts, it is impossible to doubt that St. Therese has from God a mission to fulfil in the world. But let us demonstrate that truth by several short proofs.

First, let us recall her own words. We take the word of the saints, for their virtue is the guarantee of their sincerity, and the Holy Spirit, the Spirit of Truth, abides in them and speaks through their lips. Now we know that before her death, St. Therese expressed in the clearest possible terms the mission that God had entrusted to her. "I feel," she said, "that my mission is about to commence. **My work will begin after my death. I will spend my heaven doing good upon earth."** These are only a few of her promises, among the many that might be quoted in proof of her mission after death.

Secondly, we believe in the pronouncements of the Church. In proclaiming her a saint, only twenty-eight years after her death, the Church thereby testified to the importance she attached to the cause of St. Therese and demonstrated that, in the eyes of the Church, her canonization was not solely to glorify an individual soul but to bestow a favor upon all Christendom. Moreover, her mission is amply demonstrated by this further fact that two years after her canonization the Church proclaimed her the universal patron of the missions of the Church.

Thirdly and finally, we have to believe in facts. These facts are the favors without number that she has obtained for her clients, favors so remarkable that the Holy

Father termed her "a prodigy of miracles." But God does not work miracles without reason. Above all, He does not purposely multiply miracles. A miracle, in His plan, is the letter of recommendation that He gives to His messengers to authenticate them before men; it is His seal on their works and words, and the proof of their supernatural mission. If that is true, and it is, the mission of St. Therese is indubitable. Perhaps no other saint is more divinely, more powerfully authenticated. Her mission is a reality before our eyes, for innumerable souls have received favors through her, and already walk her little way.

Given a Mission of Love

What kind of mission has God given St. Therese? Her mission is one of love. Her mission is to teach us to love God. Asked one day about the hopes that were hers as she thought of her imminent entrance into heaven, she replied: "One hope only: Love. To love, to be loved, to return to earth to make God loved." On another occasion she said: "I feel that my mission is about to commence; my mission is to make the good God loved."

Now, all the saints loved God and had an ardent desire to make Him loved; otherwise they could not have been saints. But the mission of Therese is unique in this that her work is to make God loved *as she loved Him;* that is, to teach *her little way* to us. She said: "I wish to indicate to souls the means that I found perfectly successful; to tell them that there is only one thing to do here below: to scatter for Jesus the flowers of little sacrifices, and to win Him by our caresses."

Love of God Made Easy

That is her mission given to her by God. And how clearly does not this mission manifest the inexpressible tenderness of God's love for us? For this great God so loves us and has so strong a desire for our love, that He wishes to force us, in spite of ourselves, to love Him. How force us? By rendering us altogether without excuse if we do not now love Him with all our

hearts. Because, through the little way of
St. Therese, He places the practice of divine
love, so to speak, at *our door*, and there is
not henceforth a soul howsoever feeble,
howsoever weak, who may reasonably as-
sert: "Perfection is not for me; I am too
weak, too feeble, too sinful." If you are
one of those who sometimes have protested:
"I am not at all spiritual, not at all religious as some are," learn from St. Therese
during this retreat that her little way is
easy, that it is open to all.

Fidelity in Little Things

The mission of St. Therese is in fact to
prove to the world that sanctity does not
depend upon exterior circumstances, nor
upon an abundance of natural talent, nor
upon knowledge, nor study, but only
upon love of God; and that sanctity is
acquired less by brilliant deeds than by
fidelity in little things, by a constant effort
to perform our daily duties more perfectly,
and to execute with all possible love of God
the boresome details of routine tasks with
which all our lives are filled.

Her Direct Influence upon Souls

Her mission is not only to indicate by her example the road to follow, but also to act directly upon souls to induce them to allow her to lead them to live as she did. And this not by a power exerted indirectly and from the distant heavens, but by a personal and direct apostolate within our souls. Time after time in giving novenas to the Little Flower throughout the United States, I have asked a penitent to explain his return to the sacraments after years of absence and received uniformly the answer: "I don't know, Father. That little saint got a hold on me and here I am."

A Star, an Eagle and a Dove

Doubtless she is a star which shines in the heights of heaven and from afar lights up the way, but she is also the eagle which, sighting his prey, from above the mountain peaks, swoops down, seizes it and bears it aloft. So from her high place of honor, she looks down upon us all, seeking souls whom she can make her prey and whom she can seize and bring to God. The

only defect in that metaphor is that our St.
Therese is not an eagle, but the most gentle
of doves. The amiable Little Flower takes
souls captive not by force but by her sweetness and charm.

She Descends to Sinners

She promised to come down and, faithful to her promises, she descends. No place
on earth repels or disgusts her, howsoever
low and vile it may be. We see her sometimes, often, I should say, descend to the
muddy swamps where sin and vice stagnate.
And there she speaks to those unfortunate,
fallen souls, who to us appear so loathsome
because of the mud which covers them, but
whom St. Therese finds attractive because
they are tinted with the blood of our
Saviour, shed for them.

She cries out to these souls: "The love
of God, which is my lot, shall be yours also,
if you wish. For," she says, "if I draw nigh
to God with love and trust, it is not because I have kept from mortal sin. Were
my conscience laden with every imaginable
crime, I would not have one whit less con-

fidence; heartbroken and repentant, I would throw myself into my Saviour's arms. He loves the prodigal son; I know His words addressed to Magdalen, to the adulterous woman, and to her of Samaria. Who could make me afraid? I know His mercy and His love; I know that once I had thrown myself in His arms all my numberless sins would disappear in an instant like drops of water cast into a furnace."

And in response to this touching appeal, how many souls have risen, shaken off the accumulated mud, and unfolded their wings to fly towards the heights of pure love of God! Many such souls are listening to her plea now!

She Descends to Doubters

At other times, St. Therese descends to those darkened regions of doubt, uncertainty and unbelief, searching sincere souls, for there are many such there. Into their dark night she, who on earth had been so severely tempted against faith, lets fall a ray of celestial light. To reach their minds, she ordinarily makes her entrance through their hearts. To make them believe, she first makes them love her, and to make them love her, she shows them the place where on earth she sat sympathetically at table with sinners, a voluntary victim, eating in their stead the black and bitter bread of temptation, to save them. And just as in earlier times at the call of the voice of Joan of Arc, hardened veterans rose and followed, so blasé unbelievers are now transformed and converted by the voice of Therese of Lisieux and enroll in a steady stream to march under her white banner.

She Descends to Sensualists

At other times she descends to those souls grown hard with egoism, those who falsely imagine that they will find happiness in seeking themselves and in the satisfaction of their sensual desires. She says to them: "No, happiness is not there. Happiness consists in forgetfulness of self. I myself found happiness the day that love of God entered into my heart with the message to forget myself always." Thus even in these hearts of marble, she lights first a spark and then a fire of love of God.

She Descends to Cowards

Often one sees her bend down to the cowardly and faint-hearted who dare not act manfully for God, through want of courage. She lifts them up, strengthens them, bids them hope, teaches them to be brave. She makes them understand that "one can never have too much confidence in a God so good," that "one may obtain everything from God as long as he trusts Him," that "it is confidence and nothing but confidence that leads to His love." Then she rises again to the heights, bearing on her wings those once cowardly souls now refreshed and strengthened and brave.

She Descends to the Ardent

She descends to ardent and generous souls like her own, and she inflames them by these irresistible words: "We must love Jesus as He has never before been loved."

She Descends to the Humble

She descends by preference to the humble, to those whom she sees most weak and feeble, to tell them: "So much the better, for the more weak and feeble and miserable you are, the more you need the effects of my little way and the more fit you are for it."

She Descends to All

She descends to souls who call her and to many who do not call her. She goes to many who misunderstand her, to some who have but scorn for her and her little way. Upon them she knows how to take merciful vengeance. Her revenge, after the manner of the saints, is a double portion of her affection.

The Diplomacy of Her Descent

It is thus then that she spends her heaven, catching souls in her net of love, fascinating them by her sweetness and purity. And when she has caught them under her irresistible charm, she takes advantage of her opportunity so to permeate their being that thereafter they are not able to detach themselves from her. However, St. Therese, prudent and wise, does not always show them at first the heights to which she wishes to elevate them nor the sacrifices she will demand of them to conduct them to perfection. But whatever she does demand of them, she knows how to obtain, thanks to the admirable fusion of gentleness and force which characterizes her dealing with souls.

She Leads Us to the Door of the Heart of God

It is thus that she induces souls to enter upon her little way of humility and confidence and love, and by that road she conducts them close to the heart of God. She leads them to the secret door reserved for children, a door through which none pass but *little* children, and half opening this mysterious door, she reveals to them the secrets of the love and mercy of their heavenly Father. She shows them the abyss of tenderness, even of the existence of which few souls dream—an abyss of tenderness, a furnace of love, of which the least flames

bring with them more delight than all combined earthly loves. She shows them this
open furnace of love with its flames ready
to flow over them, if they consent to let
themselves be consumed. It is enough that
they consent, for the mere desire to be a
victim is sufficient. If they consent to offer
themselves as victims of His love, impatient
to receive them, God will speedily envelop
them in His merciful love and in a very
short time will transform them into living
flames of love.

All Invited to Become Victims of His Love

What an inestimable favor that God, in
His goodness, offers not only to a few souls,
but to all who desire it, the opportunity to
become the victims of His merciful love.
Such was the ambition of St. Therese here
below and such is her ambition now in
heaven, for this was and is her prayer, with
which she closes her AUTOBIOGRAPHY:
"O Jesus, I beseech Thee to cast Thy glance
upon a vast number of little souls: I entreat
Thee to choose in this world a legion of
little *victims* worthy of Thy love."

The mission of St. Therese then is clear. It is to put into action the words of our Saviour: "I am come to cast fire on the earth and what will I but that it be kindled" (Luke 12, 49). The mission of St. Therese is to enkindle in our hearts the fire of divine love.

St. Margaret Mary and St. Therese

Thus understood, her mission is evidently a part of God's plan to reserve to these latter ages of the world the full manifestation of His Infinite mercy. The most precious and touching token of His mercy was, up to the present, the revelation of the Sacred Heart of Jesus to St. Margaret Mary. But it is also a revelation of the Divine Heart which comes to us through the humble St. Therese. In fact a beautiful comparison might be instituted between the virgin of Paray-le-Monial and the virgin of Lisieux.

St. Margaret Mary showed to the world our Saviour's Heart of *flesh,* a symbol of His love. St. Therese opened to us the depths of the heart of God in the very bosom of the adorable Trinity. The former, in manifesting the tenderness of the unprized love of the Man-God, called souls to reparation. The latter, in unveiling the paternal tenderness of the God of Mercy, invited souls to lavish upon their heavenly Father the filial tenderness consistent with our adoption as His sons and daughters. The one knows how to pluck the thorns plunged into the adorable Heart; the other knows how to cover It with flowers. The one teaches us to console; the other to delight Jesus. The one dries His tears; the other seeks to compel His smile. Thus the one and other revealed two great abysses of love or rather two doors to the same abyss. The mission of the one supplements that of the other and their glory meets in the revelation of the same Infinite Mercy. What St. Margaret Mary is to the Visitation, St. Therese is to Carmel, one of its most pure glories, not merely a star which shines but a sun which warms; not merely a radiant light but also a burning furnace of love.

Magnitude of Her Mission

The mission of St. Therese, however, is unique and singularly admirable in this, that it surpasses, by its extent, all other missions of the same kind. For she said: "I will spend my heaven doing good upon earth." Let us analyze this promise in order that we realize the extent and magnitude of her mission.

"Doing good," a noble ambition common to all great souls. But notice the astonishing addition: "I shall spend **my heaven** doing good." That is to say, in doing all the good that will be permitted her and not only from time to time but continually and unceasingly, for she adds: "I will take no rest until the angel shall have said 'Time is no more.'" There is to be no rest for her until the end of the world.

She tells us that she wishes to spend her life in heaven as our Lord spent His life on earth, for His life is summed up in the Acts of the Apostles in these two words: "doing good" (Acts 10, 38).

A Pleasing Parallel

There is a kind of parallel between the shower of roses and certain facts reported in the Gospels. The Gospels tell us that our Lord, towards the weak and troubled, towards the sick and needy, towards children and their mothers in tears, and above all towards sinners, was singularly compassionate and gentle. When He cured the sick and consoled the sorrowing, His favors were indeed precious, but His manner of bestowing them was even more touching, because it was so mild and gentle. St. Therese is gentle also when she cures and consoles, and to describe her manner of acting towards us, she makes use of an expression which poetically expresses her gentleness: "I will let fall a *shower of roses.*" As a matter of fact, her beneficent interventions sometimes are accompanied by the natural perfume of roses, but if not, they are always accomplished with exquisite grace and delicacy.

"I will spend my heaven doing good **upon earth.**" By this phrase "upon earth" she meant: throughout the world, as has been demonstrated thousands of times. When in her obscure convent cell, lying on her bed of pain, Therese pronounced these prophetic words, she often spoke with ardent desire of far distant lands where missionaries were laboring. Beneath her coarse habit, she felt beating that heart of a missionary whom her holy parents had so often implored God to give them as the last of their children. And in the ardor of her zeal she hoped to be a missionary, she tells us, not only during her short life, not only in one part of the world, but until the end of time and everywhere—wherever there would be souls to save. Her vast desires and her apparently impossible hopes were realized, for she became so active on the missions, helping, protecting, encouraging, obtaining innumerable vocations and conversions, that the bishops of all missionary countries united to petition the Holy See that she be appointed Universal Patron of the Missions of the Church and she was given that title by the decree of our present Holy Father. Although she has a *special* mission to missionary countries, the entire Church is her field; her mission and benefactions are world-wide.

The Power of a Child

Is it not astounding, by dear friends, to realize the power that God thus placed in the hands of a child? But on the other hand, is it not true that it was because she was so childlike that He gave her such power? Before God she always tried to be a child and nothing more. It was her child-like heart that caused her to conceive such far-reaching ambitions. It was her title of "child" which gave her the boldness to ask of God the realization of those dreams. It was her childlike love of Him which made her queen of the heart of God and of His power. A servant would not thus presume — nor a friend — only a child.

"Only Then Shall I Rest"

That explains why many of the *great* saints seem to finish their task with the end of their lives, and then rest in heaven. Doubtless their intercession is beneficial to the Church which continues to be inspired by the memory of their heroic virtues. But their direct action upon individual souls, although real, is not ordinarily felt sensibly.

The childlike Therese, however, commences where many of the other great saints finish, and she assures us that she will not conclude her activity or even interrupt it until the end of the world. "When the angel shall have said, 'Time is no more,' only then shall I take my repose." Nor is she content to look down on us from the heights of heaven for she said "I will come down."

"I Will Come Down"

"I will come down." Come down then during this novena, Little Flower. Come down to teach us your little way. Teach us its charm, and beauty, and the happiness there is in it. Pour out upon us the graces and favors of which God has made you mistress. Help us to practise the virtues of your little way: humility, confidence and love. Show yourself at this hour to be indeed a little queen by the royal profusion of the roses you shower upon us. Let us experience your goodness and compassion and exclude no one of us from your charity. Let there be no one amongst us, howsoever sinful in the past, whom you will fail to help. Supply to all, even to the weakest and worst sinner amongst us, courage to begin the march on your little way, relying confidently upon the boundless mercy of God, for it is your mission to teach His mercy.

"I will come down," you said. Come down then now and enter into each of our hearts and give us each the grace of graces, an ardent love of God, similar to yours. You once said: "I will work amongst souls to make Jesus King of their hearts." A king reigns, and Jesus reigns by faith and by love. Increase our faith then, O little queen, and increase our love; increase the virtues of love and faith in the hearts of all who are gathered here at your Shrine. Teach all of us here that happiness is to be found in serving God, loving Him, trusting Him, and in practising vigorously our Catholic faith. Make us understand what our religion should mean to us; what it meant to you; teach us its value, the happiness we shall find if we love our Church, love it passionately, study it, live it, practise its teachings instead of compromising with them, subtracting from them, changing them to suit ourselves.

Scatter your roses, Little Flower, during this retreat, your roses of the love of God, so that all of us will understand that without that love of God in our hearts there is no true happiness; there is no enduring peace. Dear St. Therese, little virgin of Carmel, little queen of the roses, you who are at once the apostle, the master and the masterpiece of God's love, come down today and place in each of our hearts that rose that will not wither, that rose that will not die, the rose of your own love of our Lord, of His Blessed Mother and His Church.

PART FIVE

EPILOGUE: IN WHAT SENSE ST. THERESE WAS A MARTYR

CHAPTER TEN

●

The Love of God, Which Was the Life of St. Therese, Caused Her Death

"To me, to live is Christ, and to die is gain" (Phil. 1, 21).

"At all costs I must win the martyr's palm; if not by blood, then by love" (St. Therese).

FORTY YEARS AGO TODAY, SEPTEMBER 30, 1897, the Little Flower died. For many reasons the Church chooses as the feast days of the saints the day on which they died, for the day of their death is their true birthday, being the day of their entrance into heaven, into eternal life. Six weeks before her death, August 14, 1897, St. Therese wrote to one of her missionary brothers: "I shall not die. I shall but enter into Life." That is why she wished no one to mourn her passing. "Do not weep over

126

my death," she said to her sisters, "for that would be to weep over my happiness."

Every true Christian can thus speak, for we are not like those who have no hope nor like those who have only earthly hopes, but our trust is in our Lord, Who promised eternal happiness to those who love and serve Him. The better Christians we are, the more thoroughly Christ penetrates and permeates our being, the more vast and joyful our hopes will be. "To me, to live is Christ," said St. Paul, "and to die is gain."

"To Die is Gain"

The death of a Christian is a triumph, for in God's goodness it means but a substitution, an exchange. To the faithful Christian, God exchanges this passing life in which there is so much sorrow, for an eternal life with Him in which there is no sorrow, but peace everlasting. He gives to us at death "eternal life" — life with Him, His own life. This life of God, He communicates to us first at Baptism and it rests mysteriously in our souls, under the coarse envelope of flesh which hides that "life" from our eyes, just as the splendor of the rose is concealed while it is still only a bud. But when spring comes, the bud opens and reveals the richness of the rose. Similarly when death comes, the flesh fails and the soul springs out, resplendent and overflowing with life — but with this difference, that the rose withers and dies, whereas the soul lives on eternally, and can die no more.

The death of a Christian therefore is a triumph of love, because at that hour, when faith and hope give way to the actual possession of God, love does not vanish but blooms in glory, and the soul's glory in heaven is proportioned to the degree of love it acquired on earth.

Three Kinds of Happy Deaths

There are three kinds of happy deaths, three ways in which a good Christian may die. Please notice closely these expressions: at death, one can die in God's love, or better still, for His love, or best, of His love. Let me explain.

Death In God's Love

A person dies in God's love when he dies in the grace and friendship of God. And such a death, very precious in the sight of God, suffices of course to open the gates of heaven. But it often happens that such a person's love of God is not strong enough to lead to the immediate possession of God. In that event, purgatory supplies the insufficiency. So much for a death in the love of God.

Death for God's Love

It is much better to die for the love of God. Such is the death of those who, being forced to choose between death and the denial of their faith, choose to die. Such is the death of the martyrs who, by their deaths, give supreme proof of their love, for as our Lord says: "Greater love than this no man hath than that he lay down his life for his friend." Such a death opens instantaneously the gates of heaven and leads to the immediate possession of God, without any experience of purgatory. This glorious death of a martyr is rare. Even

though at times in the history of the
Church the blood of martyrs runs in tor-
rents, nevertheless the number of martyrs
is comparatively small. All the saints were
not martyrs.

Death of God's Love

Is the glory of martyrdom then denied
to many of the saints? Is it forbidden
them? Must those, who would gladly offer
their necks to the sword of the executioner
for love of our Lord, renounce that honor
and joy and give up also all hope of giving
to their Lord the supreme proof of their
love? The Little Flower did not think so.
"At any price," she wrote to her sister,
Mother Agnes, "I must win the palm of
St. Agnes; if it cannot be by blood, I must
win it by love." She is right. Love of God
can make up for anything, supply any
want, even supply for the shedding of one's
blood, and therefore those who can not die
for love of God can die of the love of God.

What does that mean—to die of the love
of God? This is the most difficult of the
exalted truths I have tried to explain during

our novena-retreat, and I pray that I may
treat it worthily and clearly. "To die of
the love of God": that expression is difficult because unfamiliar. But we are familiar
with the other expression: "to die of grief."
Just as one may die of grief, so one can die
of the love of God. It will be helpful to
connect in your minds these two expressions: to die of grief; to die of the love of
God.

**To die of the love of God means to love
Him so much that life here below becomes
impossible.** Such a death of love can happen
in either of these two ways: (1) Either
suddenly, by the impetuosity of the desires
of a heart, which, not being able to recon-
cile itself to live so far from its Well-
Beloved God, sees its mortal bonds break
suddenly, as happened to the holy penitent
who, the same night of her conversion, died
of the very excess of her loving repentance.
(2) Or the death of the love of God may
not be sudden but come more slowly, as the
natural effect of a love of God, which causes
in the soul something similar to what the
sap and the sun cause in a fruit, which, once

ripe, detaches itself from the tree and falls. Sickness and age may, and doubtless do, help to cause such a death. But the love of the heart is a more efficient cause than the infirmity of the flesh.

There is such a thing then as a death called a death of love. Such a death was that of our Blessed Mother Mary, who is called the Queen of the Martyrs. She died of love. Separation from her divine Son she could no longer endure. Life became impossible without complete union with Him, and therefore in advance of the infirmities of old age and without any bodily sickness, she died of love. So also the Little Flower died of love. In her case, sickness helped to hasten death, but it was not so much the infirmity of the flesh as it was the love of the heart which was the principal cause of death. Such was the death she so ardently desired, for she wrote: "To die of love is a sweet martyrdom indeed and is the death I desire to suffer."

Before I can explain clearly how and in what sense St. Therese was a martyr who died of love, it will be necessary first to explain that she lived in and of the love of God. We die as we live. Our death is the echo of our life. Here, we have a vitally important lesson to learn from St. Therese. So let us place ourselves in her school to learn how, by living of the love of God, she prepared herself to die of His love.

You have often heard the expression "live on love." We say of impecunious people who marry: "They have no means; they must expect to live on love." That is exactly what the Little Flower did. She lived on love, on the love of God. To live **on** love and to live **of** love are synonymous expressions. Now by a somewhat circuitous route, let us see what we mean by saying that as some people are said to live on love, so the Little Flower lived on the love of God.

Our Loves Determine Our Lives

Man lives chiefly through his heart. It is what he loves that motivates his conduct. He lives on a level with what he loves. If what he loves is base, he lives on low levels; if what he loves is elevated, he lives on the heights. It is what he loves that determines his thoughts, his memories, his hopes and his fears, in a word, his life.

She Did Not Love Phantoms

What did the Little Flower love? Certainly not the pleasures, honors or riches of this world, for she had renounced these. She was convinced that happiness is not to be found therein. Indeed unhappy is he who (seeking happiness outside himself) is led astray by loves which do not quench, but increase his thirst, who lets himself be entirely absorbed in the love of the honors, pleasures and riches of this world. In attaching his heart to these phantoms, he hangs his happiness on dead leaves. The wind whispers and the leaves fall. Death beckons and the phantoms vanish. And his happiness? Fallen like the leaves; vanished like the phantoms.

We may well remember these figures of speech as slogans of our retreat. Do not pin your happiness to dead leaves, which any breeze will blow away. Do not depend for your happiness upon the phantoms of this world, which vanish at the approach of death.

She Did Not Love Self

Neither did St. Therese love self, for she was utterly selfless. Unhappy also is he who, filled with self, with egoism, takes as the principal occupation of his life, love of self and self-seeking, thinking only of what interests himself, thinking only of what is a cause of joy or pain to himself. "If you seek yourself," says the author of the IMITATION OF CHRIST, "you will find yourself, but it will be to your profound unhappiness." To think too much of self is to create in oneself a spring that is ever spouting turmoil and anxiety. To think too much of self is not to live in the true sense of the word; it is to live in egoism and that is no more truly to live than to pass one's life with phantoms. **The true life of man is neither outside himself with phantoms, nor inside himself with self, but inside himself with God.** That is the life a person lives who, going beyond creatures (worldly things), going beyond self, overtakes God

and binds himself to God in order to live
with God and for God. It is this life of
which St. Paul says: "You are dead and
your life is hidden with Christ in God."
(Coloss. 3, 3). In fact, to live with Christ
in God, one must first die to the life of
which we have been speaking—the sensual
and egotistical life.

She Did Not Compromise

To try, as so many do, to blend the two
kinds of life, to make a mixture, to go fifty
fifty, to live occupied with phantoms and
occupied with God, to love bagatelles and
vanities and falsehoods and at the same
time to love Eternal Truth, to be at once a
slave to the world and its caprices, and to
be at the same time a servant and friend of
Jesus Christ — is impossible — as impossible as to fix the day in the middle of the
night. It can't be done. One must **choose**.

We Must Choose Between Loves

Ah, there is a retreat slogan indeed—we
must **choose**. Sooner or later every single
soul reaches a point at which he must
choose between God and self or between

God and some creature. On his choice hangs his eternity. May St. Therese help us all to choose and to choose wisely. By choosing, I do not mean that people in the world have to choose to leave it, as the Little Flower did. Many, yes, the majority of men and women, have from God a true vocation to live in the world. But if we wish to live in the love of God, whether we are in the world or in the cloister, we must choose and our eternity depends upon our choice. Choose what? Choose to renounce all loves that are incompatible with the love of God; choose to renounce all loves forbidden by the law of God; and furthermore it is necessary to make in our hearts "a solitude," what St. Catherine of Sienna called "the interior cell," and to impose upon ourselves the obligation of living there in that solitude, in that **interior cell** alone with God, as often as is compatible with the duties of our state in life.

We Must Reflect

To live in that interior cell with God may be called "reflection"; may be called

"meditation"; may be called "prayer"; but
to retire to that solitude frequently is necessary for every one of us if we wish to live
and die in God's love. "With desolation,"
says the Holy Scripture, "is all the land
laid desolate because there is no man who
thinketh in his heart." Unless we get alone
with God and think, we shall never even
understand how far from Him or near to
Him we are; we shall never be able even to
know ourselves, nor to know whether we
are spending our lives in seeking self or
phantoms or God. Without these periods
of reflection, we shall be like the business
man who never takes inventory, never
makes up his accounts. It is to provide time
to retire into that solitude, into that interior
cell, there to be alone with God and to look
at Him and to let Him look at us, it is to
provide for this that missions are held, that
retreats for lay people are conducted, that
periods of "solitude" called "meditation"
are obligatory for religious in every religious order, in every monastery and convent in the world.

Value of Reflection

One of our most important retreat slogans and resolutions should be therefore: "To be alone with God in solitude, in our **interior cell,** to give to Him a ten-minute period of reflection at least twice a week." Otherwise we shall drift aimlessly about and never make any progress but, on the contrary, deteriorate, seeking self and phantoms without knowing we do so, pinning our happiness to dead leaves. If you never heard before of the value and necessity of these periods of reflection, it is because you never before made a retreat. To hear of it now is a grace from God, and if you act upon what you are hearing, in six months you will have made immense strides towards holiness and greater happiness. You will not be the same person you are now. Nothing has greater power of transforming a man than these prayerful periods of reflection spent alone with God.

St. Therese and Solitude

The Little Flower was definitely given to this practice of reflection even while she was in the world before entering the cloistered convent. At an age when most girls are giddy, flighty and unreflective, we find her given to periods of reflection. When she was only six, she used to retire to her bedroom and shut herself in and think. That was her solitude. Already her heart was fixed on God. Already she was beginning to live of His love. Indeed no real love of God could have developed in her without these periods of solitude in which she was alone with God, for "where thy treasure is, there is thy heart also" (Matt. 6, 21). It is a necessary consequence of human love and also of love of God that one cannot live contentedly while separated, especially for a long time, from the One Beloved. When the One Beloved is absent, He is missed; He is sought. When He is present, separation from Him is difficult and reluctant. That is why the Little Flower, even in the world, made habitually of her heart a solitude for our Lord, a solitude in which her heart could be with its Treasure and rejoice in His sweet Presence. She writes in her poem of April 30, 1896:

"My peace I find in solitude,
  Nor ask I more, dear Lord, than this:
Be thou my sole beatitude,
  And ever—in Thee—renewed
    My joy, my bliss!"

She Pondered the Gospels

Meditating upon the Gospel, she learned from our Lord's words the secret of attracting Him and His Father to her heart, for our Lord said: "If anyone love me, he shall be loved also of My Father and I will love him and *We* will come to him and will make Our abode with him" (John 14, 21-23). She seized upon these words eagerly and set herself to love Father and Son with all her heart, in order to attract Them to her, there to take up Their abode. She showed the Father the kind of love she desired to have for His Son, a love greater, stronger than had ever burned in any human heart but Mary's. She exclaimed: "O Jesus, I want so much to love Thee, to love Thee as Thou hast never been loved." And before that immense eagerness of her childlike heart, the Holy Trinity was, so to speak, helpless; that is, neither our Lord, nor the Father, nor the Holy Spirit could resist her childlike appeal. They therefore came to her, attracted by her love; They took up Their abode with her. And the same love which attracted Them, detained Them there and forbade Them to depart, and the humble Therese in triumph cried out: "O Holy Trinity, Thou art a prisoner of my love."

Her Constant Attention to God's Presence

When a soul takes captive such a Prisoner, the Prisoner is never left alone. When a person has attracted God to his heart, he does not leave God there alone and go off, distracted, inattentive to his Prisoner, preoccupied with the pursuit of self or of phantoms. No, such a person lives with God, ever contemplating, like Magdalen, His beauty, beauty ever ancient and ever new, beauty of which one never wearies nor tires. Such a person rests at the feet of our

Lord, like Magdalen, ever in His company, ever occupied in listening to Him, in admiring Him, in adoring Him and, above all, in loving Him. For to those who love, solitude is necessary, where they may commune, heart to heart. In her poem, "To Live by Love," she writes:

"To live by love—Ah! 'tis Thy life to live
   O glorious King, in whom th' elect rejoice
For me, the Host a hiding place dost give,
   For Thee to dwell in hiding is my choice.
Lovers, in solitude through day and night,
   Would linger heart to heart, and blissful rove.
Thy look, O Jesus, is my one delight,
   I live by love."

Such was the conduct of St. Therese. She occupied herself, as far as possible, solely with our Lord alone in her heart. She asked him to grant that creatures would no longer mean anything to her; that she could mean nothing to creatures; that whether they scorned her or admired her, she might not be in the least disturbed but completely indifferent; that in her eyes only Jesus would count. "His mere glance is my happiness," she said, and His mere glance was sufficient for her.

That was the beginning of her life of love of God. But the love of God has certain qualities, upon which let us now dwell, in order further to understand the heart of St. Therese, as she progressed in the love of God.

Qualities of God's Love

These are the qualities which love of God posesses: (1) It is transforming (i. e., assimilative; it produces a resemblance between the lover and the beloved). (2) It is imitative, (3) generous, (4) delicate, (5) conquering, (6) insatiable.

God's Love Transformed Her

First, love has a marvelous power to transform. For instance, two close friends, or husband and wife, often assume each other's mannerisms; and this unconsciously, by a natural tendency which friendship or love has. This the pagan sages noted centuries ago, as expressed in the ancient proverb or axiom: "Friendship always produces resemblance."

This is true of human friendship and of the friendship of God. So God's friendship transformed St. Therese and produced in her a resemblance to Him. In what way? We shall see.

Our Lord, to resemble us in all things, became man, and because He loved us, abased Himself, stripped Himself, condemned Himself to suffer as we do and to die as we do. Yes, He suffered far more than we, and died a far more painful death than will ever be our lot. Therese therefore concluded that it would be to her shame if she, who so loved our Lord, were to remain proud in the face of His humility; if she were to live a life of ease which would contrast so strangely with His life of suffering. She wanted to resemble Him Whom she loved, to resemble Him both in humility and in suffering. She says: "Oh my Beloved Jesus, Thy example invites me, in-

vites me to resemble you, to abase myself,
to humble myself, to despise honor, and
for love of Thee I will remain little and
humble and forgetting myself, I will rejoice
Thy heart." She expresses this thought in
these lines of her poem, "I Thirst for
Love":

"O my Beloved, Thy example here
   Inviteth me all honor to despise;
For Thee I would a little one appear,
   To charm Thy heart, self would I sac-
      rifice."

Imitation of Christ

Moreover, she said: "How can I be content to repose on a bed of roses when my
Beloved is nailed to the cross? How can I
sing to Thee my love in the midst of a life
of luxury, while Thou expressed Thy love
for me whilst submerged in a sea of bitter-
ness? To live of love is, on this earth, to
bear the cross. To live of love is to love
the cross. Here below then I shall, in suffering and by suffering, live of love, live in

love of Thee." Poetically she expressed this thought in this celebrated stanza:

"To live by love is not on earth to rest,
    E'en though on Thabor might our
        dwelling be;
But 'tis to *climb to Calvary's* rugged crest,
    Holding the *Cross*—our heart's sole
        treasury.
In realms celestial, joy hath endless sway,
    There trial shall no more the spirit
        prove;
But here below, in *anguish* deep I pray
    To live by love."

Generosity of Her Love of God

Love, however, is not satisfied with imitation; it calls for generosity. Its need and its joy is to give. A great soul gives everything and gives itself, its entire self. A great soul knows neither addition nor interest; nor measure nor reckoning. As the Little Flower says: "To live of love is to give without measure, without seeking reward or return; therefore I give without counting what I give because I am sure that he who loves does not know how to count."

As a matter of fact, she did give without counting. She spent herself unceasingly for our Lord. She gave everything; pains when she had them; and, when pains were lacking, she gave Him her joys. And she tells us that when she had no joys nor sorrows to offer Him, when she had nothing to give, she offered to Him that nothing, but her love made her "nothing" pleasing.

The Delicacy of Her Love

Love is also delicate. It seeks always and in everything to please the one loved. Such tenderness clothes itself in a thousand different forms, but by preference, it takes the form that pleases most the one loved. The Little Flower learned from the words of our Lord in the Gospels that nothing pleases Him more than the simple and ingenuous love of a little child. Therefore the love of a little child was, in the eyes of Therese, the ideal love to give Him. She resolved therefore to make herself a child and to remain a child until death, ever becoming more little. She would place herself in the arms of God like a very little child in the arms of a tender father. And there, banishing all fears of the past, all anxiety about the future—there she would rest, entirely trusting in Him, whether it was fair or stormy. The more reasons there were for fear, the more trust she manifested. She sought to teach us also to banish fear, when she wrote:

"To live by love is far to banish fear,
    And haunting memory of unfaithful
      days.
No shade of sin, with terror may appear;
    All is effaced in love's enkindling rays."

The darker the future appeared, the more confidence she exhibited; always trustful and always smiling, without any other occupation than to rest there near His heart, or to gather for Him the flowers of love and little sacrifices.

And because even the littleness of a child is not deaf to cries of the blasphemous and the sinful, she determined also to occupy herself there with loving atonement, to

wipe the adorable Face of her Beloved.
Therefore she sang: "To live of love is to
wipe His holy Face and to obtain for sinners pardon." In her poem, "To Live by
Love," with which I wish all would become familiar, she writes:

"To live by love is oft to soothe Thy Face,
      To win for sinners pardon and release,
O God of Love, receive them in Thy
      grace,
      And may they bless Thy name without
      surcease.
Until my heart the blasphemies repair,
      I cry a thousand times my love to prove,
I love Thee, I adore, O Name all fair,
      I live of love."

Her Love Led Her to Seek to Conquer Souls

Her love of God was also given to conquest. The greater her love of Him became,
the more she dreamed of winning other
souls who would love Him with her. That
is how she would show that she loved Him
as He had never before been loved—by
seeking, by every means in her power, to
make Him loved by a multitude, by legions

of souls, and to spend her heaven in winning over new multitudes to love Him with her. She wrote to her sister Celine: "There is but one thing to be done here below: to love Jesus, and to save souls for Him that He may be more loved." She said to her sister Pauline, later Mother Agnes: "My mission is . . . to make others love God as I love Him."

Her desire for conquest was the result of her love of our Lord, and she would win souls for God not only by her prayers and penances here but also by her activity in heaven. This activity was not to cease until the end of the world, for one day she interrupted a Sister who was speaking to her of the happiness of heaven, by these sublime words: "It is not that which attracts me." "What is it, then?" asked the Sister. "Oh! it is Love! To love, to be loved, and to return to earth to win love for our Love!"

Her Love Insatiable

What shall we say next about the life of love lived by St. Therese? It would seem that we have exhausted the subject, that we cannot analyze further her love of God. But there is more. Her love of God was insatiable, never at an end of its resources. She was ever inventing new schemes to express her love of God. Such, for instance, was her offering of herself as a victim of God's merciful love. This offering she repeated not merely thousands of times but with each beat of her heart, thus attracting to herself ever new and increasing floods of divine love.

She Died of Love

The love of God became for her what the air we breathe is to us; it became her element, her nourishment. She lived on the love of God, as we are sustained by air, and His love was the sole nourishment of her soul. It was the soul of her soul and the life of her life. Her heart beat only for the love of God. And this beating was so continual and so strong that her heart of flesh could no longer bear it and finally succumbed to the ardor of her love. Thus it came that the love of God, which was her life, was also the cause which produced her death.

Explanation of Her Death of Love

But here a question arises. How can that which gives life also produce death? If the love of God made her live, how could it also make her die? How can one die of love, by living of love?

We have here no insoluble mystery. A single comparison will clarify the matter. Think of a grain of wheat, which forms slowly, and gradually ripens. The sap that climbs up the stalk and the heat of the sun both contribute to its ripening. You have doubtless noticed the beauty of a field of ripened, golden wheat swaying gently in the sunshine. Under the sun's rays, the blade forms, then grows, then is gilded into gold, and then, if it is not harvested, it withers and drys. A day comes when the same sun which, little by little, ripened the wheat, now withers it and detaches it and separates it from the stalk. The sun which gave the wheat life, is also the cause of its death.

Love Can Cause Death

Now death is nothing else but the separation of the soul from the body. And just as the same sunshine which ripened the wheat, ends by withering it and separating it from its stalk, so divine love, which gives life to the soul, can also deal it a death blow and cause the soul's separation from the body. It does separate the soul in fact, as soon as the soul, having reached its proper perfection, under its influence, is, so to speak, ripe for the heavenly granary and has henceforth nothing more to do in its body here below.

In that sense then divine love, which gives life, can bring about death. Because divine love is the life of the soul, it tends to pull the soul away from the body. That tendency is the greater, the more ardent the love of God is. And for this reason: Although feeble, weak love of God can content itself in a narrow prison of flesh, a great love of God cannot contentedly repose there imprisoned. A real fire cannot be confined; it tends to spread and become a conflagration; it mounts to the roof and pulls down the walls that enclose it. So with divine love. A fire needs space. The human heart needs God.

Here on earth the soul, even when it possesses God by grace, cannot see Him face to face, nor possess Him fully. An obstacle intervenes—the body. "Let the body perish then," is the cry of the saints, as was the cry of St. Paul, who said: "I desire to be dissolved and to be with Christ" (Philip. 1, 23). That is to say, I desire only one thing—namely, to break down this prison of flesh to be with Christ. That is why a great heart like that of St. Therese desired death. It does more, it tries to hasten its coming, to *force* its coming.

There is another reason too why the Little Flower desires to make herself the portress to open for herself the door of death—namely, her desire to give the greatest proof of one's love, to lay down one's life for one's friend. And since there was no executioner, sword in hand, to sacrifice her life, as in the case of St. Agnes, and since there was no bonfire lighted to take away her life, as in the case of St. Joan of Arc,

the Little Flower desired that love should
replace the sword and the fire, so that she
could say to our Lord: "I love you more
than my life; I love you so much that I will
die for love of you."

She Declares Her Desire for Martyrdom

That was her dream—martyrdom. It
had been the dream of her youth, and that
dream became ever more vivid in Carmel's
narrow cell, and ended by becoming a
reality. To die of love after having lived
of love was all her life the most ardent desire of her heart. Let us listen to her as she
expresses that desire. She speaks of it in her
act of offering herself as a victim to God's
merciful love. In it, she says: "In order
that my life may be one act of perfect love,
**I offer myself as a holocaust to Thy Merciful
Love,** imploring Thee to consume me unceasingly, and to allow the floods of infinite
tenderness gathered up in Thee to overflow
into my soul, that so I may become a
martyr of Thy love, O my God!" And
then she adds: "May this martyrdom, after
having prepared me to appear before Thee,

cause me finally to die, that my soul may rush without delay into Thy eternal embrace.'''

Finally in the evening of her life, two years before she died, she writes: "To die of love is the sweetest of martyrdoms, and it is the death I desire. O Jesus, make real my dream to die of love." In her poem, "To Live by Love," she wrote:

"To die of love, 'tis martyrdom divine,
　　For which my soul thirsteth day and
　　　　night;
　O Cherubim, attune your harps with
　　　mine,
　　Full soon from exile shall my soul take
　　　　flight;
　O burning dart, consume me with thy fire,
　　Wound thou my heart, as lonely here
　　　I sigh,
　O Jesus, grant my dream, my one desire—
　　　Of love to die."

And the last stanza of this poem begins with these lines:

"To die of love, ah! 'tis my hope most dear,
　　When shalt Thou break these fleeting
　　　ties of earth."

The Two Death Forces

Let us penetrate further into this touching mystery. Let us recall that grain of wheat which ripens. A double action was exerted upon it and tended to separate it from its stalk; one force operated from within (its sap), the other from without (the sun); the sap fertilized it and the sun warmed it.

Likewise in the Little Flower, who aspired to die of divine love, there were **two forces** which, combining their action, tended to separate the soul from the body: on the one hand, the soul itself which, with all the ardor of its desires, tended towards God; and on the other hand God, Who, with all the power of His love, tended to unite Himself to that soul. Let us watch these two forces at work in the soul of St. Therese.

Although she desired, like St. Paul, to die and to be with Christ, her desire was conditional, dependent upon our Lord's wish. For she desired His pleasure more than death, more than life. "Certainly I will remain here below and gladly as long as He wishes, but if He too should desire my death . . . "

And He did desire it, for He made known His desire to her. What evidence have we for this statement?

The Evidence

One day, two years before her death, when still in the robust health of a normal girl of twenty-two, she felt a presentiment of her approaching death. She tells us in the thirteenth chapter of her AUTOBIOGRAPHY that she understood from Him that He would not leave her long on earth. "I do not say that it will be immediately," she explains, "but two or three years at the latest."

Then came what she terms the first distant call of her Beloved, which came just after midnight, Holy Thursday, 1897. To use her own words, "Scarcely had I laid my head on the pillow when I felt a hot stream rise to my lips, and **thinking I was going to die,** my heart almost broke with joy. I had already put out our lamp, so I mortified my curiosity till morning and went peacefully to sleep.

"At five o'clock, the time for rising, I remembered immediately that I had some **good news** to learn, and going to the window I found, as I had expected, that our handkerchief was saturated with blood. What hope filled my heart! I was firmly convinced that on the anniversary of His death my Beloved had allowed me to hear His first call, like a sweet distant murmur, heralding His joyful approach."

Her Wound by the Fiery Dart

Then came another sign still more sure —what is called "her wound by a dart of divine love." "I had commenced the Stations of the Cross in the chapel, when all at once I felt myself wounded by a dart of fire so ardent that I thought I must die. I do not know how to explain it; it was as if an invisible hand had plunged me wholly into fire. Oh, what fire and what sweetness at the same time. I was burning with love; I was being burnt by a veritable flame, and I thought one minute, nay, one second more and I shall not be able to support such ardor without **dying**."

As a matter of fact, her heart did give way under the mysterious wound it had suffered and she fell senseless upon the floor of the chapel. But it was all over in a moment. Our Lord had withdrawn the spear before it caused death. But it had left a mortal wound, of which her heart was not to be cured.

She Seeks to Hasten Death

Henceforth Therese could not misunderstand the intentions of her Divine Spouse. Indeed the hour was approaching when she would spring into His arms. Thinking to respond to the desire of our Lord, she asked permission to die from the Mother Prioress. Carmelite nuns thus carry obedience to what appears to worldly souls to be ridiculous extremes and ask of their superiors permission to die. The permission was refused her. But her illness progressed slowly, too slowly in spite of her desires that death come quickly. She could not but at times confess that she found this sickness, of which she was dying, a guide all too slow in leading her to death's door. Therefore

she made use of strategy. She was not of
course permitted to hasten her death, but
was she forbidden, she asked herself, to
recall to our Lord His own words? She
did not forget that our Lord, speaking of
sudden death, compares Himself to a thief
who comes when He is least expected, and
therefore she said: "If He should come
very soon to steal me, I would help Him
very much." On another occasion she said:
"I know that God desires a little cluster
of grapes which no one will give Him and
which therefore He will be obliged to come
and steal. I see Him and I take good care
not to cry 'Thief,' but on the contrary I
call Him, saying, 'Here it is—here.' "

It was by such tender strategy and delicate finesse of love that she sought to hasten
the hour when her Divine Spouse would
come to take her and unite Himself to her
eternally.

She Desired the Death of the Cross

But, my dear friends, do not allow the
charm of these sentiments to deceive you,
for these words were not merely the poetic

expression of a tender soul. The poetic quality is there, but behind it was no mawkish sentimentality but solid faith and ardent love which was not content with words but sought expression in deeds and in sacrifice, for she says: "The death of love I desire is that of Jesus **on the cross.**"

We know how He died, with what agony and suffering. One day St. Therese remarked: "The martyrs died joyfully, but the King of Martyrs in sadness, and I want to die His death." Let us see what her death was. For a long time before her death, there were painful temptations against faith. A wall of temptation rose between her soul and heaven, which was divested of all its charms. But she preferred it thus since God willed it, in order that in her death, as in her life, there would be no personal satisfaction. To die without joy was her desire. But the death of our Lord was not only empty of joy but filled, saturated with pain and agony. She wished to love Him as He had loved her; she aspired therefore to give Him love for love, and if possible, pain for pain, and to die as

He died. Her wish was so far granted that on her death bed she often exclaimed: "I did not think it possible to suffer so much." The darkness, the temptations, the pains of her agony, held both her soul and body in a vise-like grip, so that she more than once exclaimed: "It is pure agony, pure agony"; and then added: "But I would not have it otherwise, I would not suffer less."

Details of Her Death

Let Mother Agnes, her sister Pauline, tell the story of the last moments of St. Therese. Her description appears in the epilogue to the AUTOBIOGRAPHY and reads as follows:

"Looking at her crucifix she continued: 'Oh ... I love Him! ... My God, I ... love ... Thee!' These were her last words. It was now a quarter past seven, and her terrible agony of body and soul had lasted for fully twelve hours. Scarcely had she spoken, when to our great surprise her whole frame drooped quite suddenly, the head inclined a little to the right, in the attitude of the

Virgin Martyrs offering themselves to the sword; or as a Victim of Love, awaiting from the Divine Archer the fiery shaft by which she longs to die. All at once she raised herself, as though called by a mysterious voice, and opening her eyes, which shone with unutterable joy, she fixed her gaze a little above the statue of Our Lady."

Her look of ecstasy seemed to say: "Oh. how beautiful; more beautiful than I have ever dreamed!" This ecstasy of love lasted but a few moments and then the soul of little Therese, carried by the Divine Eagle, disappeared in the heights of the heavens.

"I shall not die," she had said, "I shall but enter into life. And whatsoever I cannot tell you here on earth, I will make you understand from the heights of heaven."

O dear little saint, during this novena commemorating the anniversary of your death and of your entrance into heaven, fulfil now for all of us that promise of yours. Make us *understand* that your life and your death prove beyond all manner of doubt that which we poor worldlings find difficulty in *understanding*—namely, that, as you said, there is but one thing to do here below: to love our Lord and to save our souls and those of others, so that He may also be loved by them.

Make us *understand* that, when all is said and done, in life as in death nothing matters, nothing counts, except the love of God; that everything else may be lacking to us, but if we possess His love, then in reality we lack nothing.

For this love of God, of which you lived and of which you died, give us hunger; for it, give us thirst; grant we may not be content to live in His love and friendship but that we aspire, and *ardently* aspire to live, as you did of His love.

And since on their feast days the queens of earth are bountiful with their gifts, so do you, little heavenly queen, refuse us nothing today that will be good and useful for our souls. Give to us of your treasures, of the treasures of God of which He has made you mistress. Shower your roses upon all of us who are petitioning you: roses of consolation, roses of relief from suffering, roses of health and peace. But give also those roses which many do not dream of asking but which are the most precious of all, the true roses of heaven: faith, confidence, the spirit of sacrifice, forgetfulness of self, humility and, above all, love of God. Yes, place in all our hearts a great, immense love of God, so that at this end of our novena, we shall not depart with empty souls, but, on the contrary, with souls overflowing with heavenly riches.

We do not want roses that fade and wither, nor do you, dear St. Therese, desire to give such roses to us. Give us therefore the rose that you so loved, the rose that grew in your soul, the rose that is planted in the intimacy of the heart, and takes root there in order to bloom, gorgeous and imperishable, on the day eternity dawns. Dear little saint, masterpiece of divine love, place in all our hearts that rose of the Love of God. In and of that love grant that we live, and in and of that love grant that we may die.

MOTHER by Kathleen Norris   Fiction

The original Pro-Life novel...Over 7 million copies in print!

"Such was our enthusiasm after reading this book that we longed to place it in the hands of all mothers and grown daughters of our land." — Catholic World

A timeless coming-of-age classic which finds the novel's heroine, Margaret Paget, experiencing a restless longing for adventure and a need to escape the small New York town where she grew up and now teaches school. She dearly loves her mother, the real champion of the story, but is convinced she must rise above the drudgery of her poor mother's daily life. Inspiring.

5¼ x 7½   172 pages softcover $9.95

THE NUN by René Bazin   Fiction

This is the tragic story of five nuns abruptly cast back into the secular world during turn-of-the-century Lyons, France. Betrayed by her government and her family, one young nun, Pascale Mouvand, is on the verge of losing hope in God's loving nature when the prayers of her fellow sisters call forth an infusion of God's grace into her soul.

"It is the epic of the persecuted church, terrible in its truth, terrible in its portent, terrible in its indictment."—The Monitor

5¼ x 7½   243 pages softcover $10.95

The Immaculate Heart of Mary

DEVOTIONAL

By John Peter Pinamonti

For those who like a little history to their book! This book is the fruit of thirty-eight years of missionary work beginning in northern Italy in 1665!

Divided into 7 considerations
—one for each day of the week!

With the help of over forty Fathers, Doctors, ecclesiastical writers and mystics of the church, including St. Anselm, St. Thomas Aquinas, St. Bridget of Sweden, St. Augustine, and St. Catherine of Siena, Father Pinamonti helps readers understand the nature and meaning of Our Lady's Immaculate Heart. His crystal clearness of thought and expression brings us a spirit-filled book perfect for the simple soul wanting to achieve a better understanding of the essentials of Christian piety.

Perfect companion volume for souls consecrated to Our Lady's Immaculate Heart!

4¼ x 7 144 pages, softcover $8.95

To order please send check or money order to St. Michael's Press, 229 North Church Street, #400, Charlotte, NC 28202 or call 1-800-933-9398. Please include $3.00 for shipping & handling for the first book; 75¢ for each additional book. NC residents add 6% to retail total for state tax.